Bible Truths

Arranged and Copyrighted
by
The late Alva J. McClain, Th.M., D.D., LL.D.
Founder and First President
Grace Theological Seminary
Winona Lake, Indiana

BMH Books
www.bmhbooks.com

MW01037264

Fourteenth printing, June 2008

Copyright 1950, Alva J. McClain
Copyrght 1979, BMH Books

ISBN: 978-0-88469-013-9

RELIGION / Christian Theology / General

BMH BOOKS
Winona Lake, Indiana

Printed in U.S.A.

CONTENTS

Introduction

This little booklet, which has been out of print for several years, was originally prepared during a busy pastorate to provide some systematic doctrinal instruction for our own Sunday school. Although the first edition was limited in number, a few congregations used it in Church School and Christian Endeavor work. Also it was translated into Spanish, French, and two African languages for use in mission fields. In response to frequent requests, this revised and enlarged edition has been prepared.

A few explanatory notes should be made. First, the catechetical method has been retained; and all answers to the questions, with but one or two exceptions, are direct quotations from the Bible. Thus the student need memorize nothing but the Word of God. Second, except in a few instances where it seemed necessary, all comment and notations have been avoided. Third, as a general rule quotations are taken from the Authorized Version. When the American Standard Revised Version is used, the reference is marked "ASV." Fourth, in all passages where the name "Holy Ghost" occurs, it is changed to "Holy Spirit." The former name unfortunately, to the minds of children, has a superstitious connotation. Fifth, in some instances a portion of the Biblical passage has been omitted. This was done only to shorten the quotation, not to misrepresent its meaning. In every such case the omission is properly indicated.

It is sincerely hoped that "BIBLE TRUTHS" will serve in some measure a threefold purpose; as a little handbook of Christian doctrine for all members of the church; for that catechetical instruction which is so sorely needed by the children of our Sunday schools; and also as an elementary guide for use in adult Bible classes or prayer meeting. With this last purpose in mind, considerable time and labor have been spent in selecting and adding lists of important supplementary references which bear upon the various doctrines treated. The student will find all of them worth looking up. Even the order of their arrangement will often be found significant.

For those who desire to use the booklet in Bible classes, the following suggestions may be of some value. First, if possible, get the students to look up in their Bibles the extra references before coming to the class, and select the best one. Second, as the passages are read in class, insist upon keeping to the point under discussion in each question. Often inquiries will arise which are dealt with under a later question. It will be found helpful to have the students mark in their Bibles the **word** or **phrase** which bears directly on the question. Third, the lists of references, while very carefully chosen, are not exhaustive. On certain subjects the teacher may wish to add others, and should encourage the class to do the same. Before doing this under any particular question, however, the teacher should look over the chapter carefully to see whether the suggested references are not used under later questions. Thus repetition will be avoided. Fourth, it will be profitable to open the class by reading responsively the chapter to be studied. All members of the Sunday school, during my pastorate in the First Brethren Church, of Philadelphia, were furnished with copies so that it could be used for responsive reading in the opening exercises at certain times.

When used for memory work in children's classes, teachers should go through the booklet and mark one or more questions in each chapter, being careful to select those which will be clear to the child and which are answered by verses easily committed to memory. For examples, see Question 2 in Chapter 1, and 14 in II. A certain number could be required for graduation from the various departments of the Sunday school, the number being increased to suit the ages and ability.

Only those who may have attempted to prepare a work of this kind will realize how much painstaking labor is involved. The very wealth of Biblical material was embarrassing. And now, reading the completed manuscript, I can see many places where it might be improved and strengthened. To write a book, I think would have been easier. But the task was not unpleasant, and the result is once more offered to all who love the "Word of Truth" with a humble prayer that "our great God and Saviour Jesus Christ" may graciously use it to instruct us more fully in that Blessed Word which reveals His Unspeakable Glory, that we might indeed be sanctified in the Truth.

Alva J. McClain
Winona Lake, Indiana.

I. THE BIBLE

1. **What name does the Bible give to its own writings?**
   "The Holy Scriptures"—II Timothy 3:15.
   (Dan. 10:21; Mark 7:13; Rom. 3:2;10:8; Eph. 1:13; Phil. 2:16; Col. 3:16; II Thess. 3:1; Heb. 5:13; 6:5

2. **Who gave us the Scriptures?**
   "All Scripture is given by inspiration of God"—II Timothy 3:16.
   (Exod. 20:1; I Thess. 2:13; Heb. 1:1)

3. **Through whom did God give the Scriptures?**
   "Holy men of God spake as they were moved by the Holy Spirit"—II Peter 1:21.
   (Exod. 24:4; II Sam. 23:1-2; Jer. 36:1-4; Joel 1:1; I Cor. 14:37; Rev. 1:1-2, 9-10)

4. **Prove that the very words of the Bible are from God.**
   "Which things also we speak, not in the WORDS which man's wisdom teacheth, but which the Holy Spirit teacheth"—I Corinthians 2:13.
   (Exod. 4:10-12; Prov. 30:5; Jer. 1:6-9; 30:1-2: John 8:47)

5. **What did our Lord teach about the Scriptures?**
   "Thy Word is truth"—John 17:17. "The Scripture cannot be broken"—John 10:35.
   (Psa. 33:4; 119:89, 160; Matt. 5:18; 24:35: Mark 14:49: I Pet. 1:25)

6. **Did Christ believe everything taught in the Scriptures?**
   "Verily I say unto you, Till heaven and earth pass, one jot or one tittle shall in no wise pass from the Law, till ALL be fulfilled"—Matthew 5:18.
   (Matt. 12:40 Luke 4:25, 27; 17:27, 29; John 3:14)

7. **Should we believe all the Scriptures as Christ believed them?**
   "Let this mind be in you, which was also in Christ Jesus"—Philippians 2:5.
   (Luke 24:25; John 13:16)

8. **What should we do with the Bible?**
   "Blessed is he that READETH, and they that HEAR

the words of this prophecy, and KEEP those things which are written therein"—Revelation 1:3.

(Deut. 6:6-7; Ps. 119:97; John 2:22; Acts 17:11; Phil. 2:16; II Thess. 3:14; II Tim. 2:15; 4:2; James 1:22)

9. What great Person will we find in the Scriptures, if we search them?

"Search the Scriptures . . . they are they which testify of Me"—John 5:39.

(Luke 24:27, 44-45; John 5:46; Acts 8:26-35; 10:43)

10. Why were the Scriptures written?

"These are written that ye might believe that Jesus is the Christ, the Son of God; and that believing ye might have life through His Name"—John 20:31.

(I Cor. 10:11; II Tim. 3:16-17; I John 1:4; 2:1)

11. What will the Bible do for us if we read and believe it?

"The Holy Scriptures . . . are able to make thee wise unto salvation through faith which is in Christ Jesus"—II Timothy 3:15.

(Psa. 19:7; 119:11, 130; John 15:3; Acts 20:32; Rom. 10:17; I Thess. 4:18; Heb. 4:12; I Pet. 1:23; II Pet. 3:18)

12. To what is the Bible compared?

"As newborn babes, desire the sincere MILK of the Word, that ye may grow thereby"—I Peter 2:2.

(Ps. 119:103, 105; Isa. 55:10-11; Jer. 23:29; Luke 8:11; Eph. 5:26; 6:17; Heb. 5:12-14)

13. What will happen to those who take a wrong attitude toward God's Word?

"Whoso despiseth the Word shall be destroyed" —Proverbs 13:13.

(Jer. 12:17; Mark 8:38; John 12:48; II Thess. 1:7-8, 2:11-12; Heb. 2:1-3; Rev. 22:18-19)

14. What should be our prayer as we read the Word of God?

"Open Thou mine eyes, that I may behold wondrous things out of Thy law"—Psalm 119:18.

(Ps. 119:33-36, 38, 133; Eph. 1:17; Col. 1:9)

II. GOD

1. **Why should all men know that there is a God?**
   "The heavens declare the glory of God; and the firmament sheweth His handywork"—Psalm 19:1.
   (Job 12:7-9; Ps. 19:2-4; Acts 14:17; Rom. 1:19-20)

2. **How does the Bible speak of those who say there is no God?**
   "The FOOL hath said in his heart, There is no God"—Psalm 14:1.
   (Job 8:11-13; Psa. 10:4 ASV; 36:1; Rom. 1:28; II Tim. 2:12; Heb. 11:6)

3. **Are there more Gods than one?**
   "I am the Lord, and there is none else; there is no God beside Me"—Isaiah 45:5.
   (Deut. 6:4-5; Isa. 44:6-8; Mark 12:29-30; John 5:44 ASV; 10:30)

4. **What Persons are in the one true God?**
   "The Father . . . the Son . . . the Holy Spirit"—Matthew 28:19.
   (Each is called God—John 6:27; Acts 5:3-4; Rom. 9:5) (cf. Isa. 48:16; 61:1; John 14:26; 15:26; II Cor. 13:14; Eph. 2:18; 4:4-6; I Pet. 1:2)

5. **What kind of a Being is God?**
   "God is a SPIRIT; and they that worship Him must worship Him in spirit and in truth"—John 4:24.
   (What is "spirit"?—Luke 23:46; 24:39; John 3:5-8; 6:63; Rom. 8:11; James 2:26)

6. **Has anyone ever seen God as a spirit?**
   "No man hath seen God at any time"—John 1:18.
   (John 6:46; Col. 1:15; I Tim. 1:17; 6:16; Heb. 11:27; I John 4:12)

7. **How is it possible for us to see God?**
   "Philip saith unto Him, Lord, shew us the Father . . . Jesus saith unto him . . . He that hath seen ME hath seen the Father"—John 14:8-9.
   (John 1:14, 18; 12:45-46; II Cor. 4:6; Col. 1:15; 2:9; Heb. 1:3)

8. What does the Bible teach about the Life of God?
"The Lord is the true God; He is the LIVING GOD"—Jeremiah 10: 10.
(Ps. 36:9; Jer. 2:13; Dan. 6:26; John 5:26; I Thess. 1:9)

9. What does the Bible teach about the Eternity of God?
"Before the mountains were brought forth, or ever Thou hadst formed the earth and the world, even from everlasting to everlasting Thou art God" —Psalm 90:2.
(Gen. 21:33; Deut. 33:27; Dan. 4:34; Rev. 4:10)

10. What does the Bible teach about the Knowledge of God?
"God is greater than our heart, and knoweth all things"—I John 3:20.
(Job 28:24; 37:16; Ps. 139:1-4; 147:4; Prov. 15:3; Matt. 10: 29; Acts 15:18; I John 1:5)

11. What does the Bible teach about the Presence of God?
"Whither shall I flee from Thy presence? If 1 ascend up into heaven, Thou art there: if I make my bed in hell, behold, Thou art there. If I take the wings of the morning, and dwell in the uttermost parts of the sea, even there shall Thy hand lead me, and Thy right hand shall hold me"—Psalm 139: 7-10.
(I Kings 8:27; Jer. 23:23-24; John 14:23; Acts 17:27-28)

12. What does the Bible teach about the Power of God?
"Lord God, behold, Thou hast made the heaven and the earth by Thy great power and stretched out arm, and there is nothing too hard for Thee"—Jeremiah 32:17.
(Gen. 17:1; Job. 42:1-2; Isa. 40:28; Dan. 4:35; Matt. 19:26; Rev. 19:6)

13. What does the Bible teach about the Holiness of God?
"Holy, holy, holy, is the Lord of hosts: the whole earth is full of His glory"—Isaiah 6:3.
(Lev. 27:28; Deut. 26:15; Psa. 47:8; 98:1; 99:1-9; 105:42; Isa. 57:15; I Pet. 1:15-16)

14. What does the Bible teach about the Love of God?
"For God so loved the world, that He gave His only begotten Son, that whosoever believeth in Him should not perish, but have everlasting life" —John 3:16.

(Deut. 7:7-8; Isa. 63:9; Jer. 31:3; John 17:24; Rom. 5:8; I John 3:1; 4:7-11, 19)

15. What does the Bible teach about the Truth of God?
"And this is life eternal, that they might know Thee the only TRUE God, and Jesus Christ whom Thou hast sent"—John 17:3.

(Psa. 31:5; 91:4;117:2; 119:151; John 17:17; Rom. 2:2; Titus 1:2)

16. What does the Bible teach about the Righteousness of God?
"The Lord is RIGHTEOUS in all His ways, and holy in all His works"—Psalm 145:17.

(Psa. 11:7; 19:8; 92:15; Acts 17:31; Rom. 3:35-26; Heb. 6:10; Rev. 16:5-7)

17. What does the Bible teach about the Goodness of God?
"O give thanks unto the Lord, for He is GOOD; for His mercy endureth for ever"—Psalm 136:1.

(Psa. 25:8; 31:19; 33:5; 34:8; 65:11-13; 68:9-10; 86:5; 145:9; Rom. 2:4)

18. What does the Bible teach about the Faithfulness of God?
"Know therefore that the Lord thy God, He is God, THE FAITHFUL GOD, which keepeth covenant and mercy with them that love Him and keep His commandments to a thousand generations" —Deuteronomy 7:9.

(Psa. 36:5; 89:33; 119:90; I Cor. 1:9; 10:13; I Thess. 5:23-24; II Thess. 3:3; I John 1:9)

19. What does the Bible teach about the Provision of God?
"Nevertheless He left not himself without witness, in that He did good, and gave us rain from heaven, and

fruitful seasons, filling our hearts with food and gladness"—Acts 14:17.

(Deut. 11:13-17; Psa. 27-28; 65:9-13; 104:10-14; 145:15-16; Matt. 5:44-45)

20. What does the Bible teach about the Wrath of God?

"For the wrath of God is revealed from heaven against all ungodliness and unrighteousness of men"—Romans 1:18.

(Psa. 2:10-12; 90:11; Isa. 13:9, 11, 13; John 3:36 with Rev. 15:7; Eph. 5:6; I Thess. 1:10; 5:9; Rev. 6:12-17)

21. Does God ever change in His character?

"For I am the Lord, I CHANGE NOT"—Malachi 3:6.

(Exod 3:14; Num. 23:19; Ps. 33:11; Ezek. 24:14; James 1:17)

22. What does the Bible teach about the Perfection of God?

"He is the Rock, His work is PERFECT . . . a God of truth and without iniquity, just and right is He"—Deuteronomy 32:4.

(Job 37:16; Psa. 18:30; 19:7; 138:8; Rom. 12:2; James 1:17)

23. Are we able to understand everything about God?

"O, the depth of the riches both of the wisdom and knowledge of God! How unsearchable are His judgments, and His ways past finding out"—Romans 11:33.

(Job 5:8-9; 11:7-9; Ps. 145:3; Isa. 40:28)

24. What does a man worship when he turns away from the true God?

"HE MAKETH A GOD . . . he falleth down unto it, and worshippeth it, and prayeth unto it, and saith, Deliver me, for thou art my god"—Isaiah 44:17.

(Deut. 32:17; Rom. 1:21-25; I Cor. 10:20; Rev. 9:20)

III. JESUS CHRIST

1. **What are some of the names given to our Lord Jesus Christ in the Bible?**

   "His name shall be called Wonderful, Counselor, The Mighty God, The Everlasting Father, The Prince of Peace"—Isaiah 9:6.

   (Mal. 4:2; Matt. 20:28; John 1:29; 3:18; 10:11; 13:13; Acts 3:15; Heb. 4:14; Rev. 19:13, 16; 22:16)

2. **What did the Lord Jesus teach about His existence before He was born in Bethlehem?**

   "And now, O Father, glorify Thou Me with Thine own self with the glory which I had with Thee before the world was"—John 17:5.

   (Mic. 5:2; John 1:15; 6:62; 8:57-58; 16:28-30; I Cor. 10:4, 9; Phil. 2:6-7; Col. 1:17)

3. **What does the Bible teach about the Birth of Christ?**

   "Behold, A VIRGIN shall be with child, and shall bring forth a Son; and they shall call His Name Emmanuel, which being interpreted is, God with us"—Matthew 1:23.

   (Gen. 3:15; Isa. 7:14; Matt. 1:18-25; Luke 1:26-35; 2:1-14; Rom. 1:3; Gal. 4:4)

4. **How does the Bible teach that Jesus Christ is God?**

   "In the beginning was the Word, and the Word was with God, and the Word was God"—John 1:1.

   (John 5:17-18, 23; 20:28-29; Rom. 9:5; Col. 2:9; Titus 2:13; Heb. 1:6, 8; 13:8; I John 5:20)

5. **What are some of the works of Christ which show that He is God?**

   "All things were made by Him, and without Him was not anything made that was made—John 1:3.

   (Mark 2:5-7; John 10:28, 14:14; 5:21-22; Heb. 1:3)

6. **What are some of our Lord's claims for Himself, which prove that He is God?**

   "I am the Way, the Truth, and the Life; no man

cometh unto the Father, but by Me"—John 14:6.

(Matt. 11:28; John 6:35; 7:37; 8:12; 10:9; 10:14 with Ps. 23:1; John 11:25; 15:5; 16:15)

7. **Prove that our Lord also became a real human being by His birth into the world.**

"Wherefore IN ALL THINGS it behoved Him to be made like unto His brethren, that He might be a merciful and faithful high priest"—Hebrews 2:17.

(Matt. 4:2; Luke 2:40, 52; John 4:6; 11:35; 19:28; I Cor. 15:47; Heb. 5:8)

8. **What does the Bible teach about the wonderful works of Christ while He was on earth?**

"God anointed Jesus of Nazareth with the Holy Spirit and with power: Who went about DOING GOOD, and healing all that were oppressed of the devil; for God was with Him"—Acts 10:38.

(Matt. 4:23; 11:20; 13:58; Luke 2:49; John 5:36; 9:4; 10:32; 17:4)

9. **Did our Lord ever do anything wrong or sinful?**

"And ye know that He was manifested to take away our sins; and in Him is NO SIN"—I John 3:5.

(John 8:46; Acts 3:14; II Cor. 5:21; Heb. 4:15; 7:26-27; I Pet 1:19; 2:22)

10. **Why was our Lord born into the world as a Man?**

"This is a faithful saying, and worthy of all acceptation, that Christ Jesus came into the world TO SAVE SINNERS; of whom I am chief"—I Timothy 1:15.

(John 1:14; 10:10; II Cor. 8:9; Gal. 4:4-5; I Pet. 2:21)

11. **What did Christ do to save sinners?**

"Christ died for our sins according to the Scriptures"—I Corinthians 15:3.

(Isa. 53:5-8; Matt. 20:28; Mark 8:31; John 10:10, 17-18: 12:23-24; Rom. 5:6-8)

12. **How did Christ suffer and die for our sins?**

"And when they were come to the place, which is called Calvary, there they CRUCIFIED Him"—Luke 23:33.

(Ps. 22:14-18; Matt. 27:26-31; Mark 15:29-34; John 19:2835; Acts 2:23)

13. What did the death of our Lord do for all who believe on Him?

"Christ hath redeemed us from the curse of the law, being made a curse for us; for it is written, Cursed is everyone that hangeth on a tree"—Galatians 3:13.

(John 6:51; Rom. 5:9-10; II Cor. 5:15, 21; Eph. 2:12-13, Gal. 1:4; I Thess. 5:10; Heb. 10:10; I Pet. 1:18-19; 2:24; Rev. 1:5)

14. What great thing took place three days after Christ died?

"God raised Him from the dead; and He was seen many days of them which came up with Him from Galilee to Jerusalem, who are His witnesses unto the people"—Acts 13:30-31.

(Ps. 16:8-10; Isa. 53:10; Matt. 28:1-10; Mark 9:31; Acts 4:33; Rev. 1:18)

15. How did our Lord prove that His body was raised from the dead?

"He showed Himself alive after His passion BY MANY INFALLIBLE proofs, being seen of them forty days, and speaking of the things pertaining to the Kingdom of God"—Acts 1:3.

(Luke 24:36-43; John 20:24-29; I Cor. 15:3-8)

16. Why is the Resurrection of Christ important to us?

"Blessed be the God and Father of our Lord Jesus Christ, which according to His abundant mercy hath begotten us again unto a lively [living] hope by the Resurrection of Jesus Christ from the dead"—I Peter 1:3.

(John 2:18-21; 14:19; Acts 17:30-31; Rom. 1:4; 4:25; 6:8-9; 14:9; I Cor. 15:14-20)

17. Where did Christ go after His Resurrection?

"And it came to pass, while He blessed them, He was parted from them, and carried up INTO HEAVEN" —Luke 24:51.

(Mark 16:19; John 6:62; Acts 1:9; Eph. 1:20-21; 4:8-10)

18. What is Christ doing now in heaven?"

"For Christ is not entered into the holy places made with hands, which are the figures of the true; but into heaven itself, now to appear in the presence of God for us"—Hebrews 9:24.

(John 14:2; Acts 2:33; Heb. 4:14-16; 6:20; 8:1; 10:12-13; I John 2:1)

19. Will our Lord ever come back from heaven to earth?

"This same Jesus, which is taken up from you into heaven, shall so come in like manner as ye have seen Him go into heaven"—Acts 1:11.

(John 14:1-3; I Thess. 4:15-18; Heb. 9:28; Rev. 1:7. For other references see chapter on "Second Coming")

20. Since Christ has done so much for us, how should we show our gratitude?

"For ye are bought with a price; therefore glorify God in your body, and in your spirit, which are God's"—I Corinthians 6:20.

(John 13:34; 14:15; Eph. 5:2; Col. 3:1-2, 13; I Pet. 2:21-22; I John 2:6)

NOTES

IV. THE HOLY SPIRIT

1. **What promise concerning the Holy Spirit did our Lord make just before He ascended into heaven?**

   "I will pray the Father, and He shall give you another Comforter, that He may abide with you for ever; even the Spirit of Truth, whom the world cannot receive"—John 14:16-17.

   (John 7:39; 16:7; Acts 2:1-4; 2:33)

2. **How does the Bible speak of the Holy Spirit as a real Person?**

   "Howbeit when HE, the Spirit of Truth, is come, HE WILL GUIDE you into all truth: for He shall not speak of Himself; but whatsoever HE SHALL HEAR, that SHALL HE SPEAK; and HE WILL SHOW you things to come"—John 16:13.

   (Acts 132; Rom. 8:27; 15:30; I Cor. 2:13; 12:11)

3. **How does the Bible teach that the Holy Spirit is God?**

   "But Peter said, Ananias, why hath Satan filled thine heart to lie to the HOLY SPIRIT? . . . Thou hast not lied unto men, but unto God"—Acts 5:34.

   (Ps. 139:7; Matt. 28:19; II Cor. 13:14; Heb. 9:14)

4. **What special work does the Holy Spirit have in Nature?**

   "By His Spirit He hath garnished the heavens"—Job 26:13.

   (Gen. 1:2-3; Ps. 104:29-30; Isa. 32:15; 40:7)

5. **What special work did the Holy Spirit have in Christ's life on earth?**

   "God anointed Jesus of Nazareth with the Holy Spirit and with power: who went about doing good"—Acts 10:38a.

   (Matt. 3:16; Luke 1:34-35; 4:1-2; Rom. 8:11; Heb. 9:14)

6. **What special work does the Holy Spirit have in relation to the Bible?**

   "For the prophecy came not in old time by the will of

man: but holy men of God spake as they were moved by the Holy Spirit"—II Peter 1:21.

(II Sam. 23:1-2; John 16:12-13; I Cor. 2:11-13; Eph. 6:17; Rev. 3:22)

7. **What special work does the Holy Spirit have in the unsaved world?**

"When He is come, He will reprove [convict] the world of sin, and of righteousness, and of judgment: of sin, because they believe not on Me; of righteousness, because I go to My Father, and ye see Me no more; of judgment, because the prince of this world is judged"—John 16:8-11.

(Gen. 6:3, 5; John 15:26; II Thess. 2:7-8 ASV, Heb. 3:7)

8. **What special work does the Holy Spirit have in our salvation?**

"Not by works of righteousness which we have done, but according to His mercy He saved us, by the washing of regeneration, and renewing of the Holy Spirit"—Titus 3:5.

(John 3:5; I Cor. 6:11; 12:3; Eph. 1:13 ASV)

9. **Prove that since Pentecost all true Believers have the Baptism of the Holy Spirit.**

"For in one Spirit were WE ALL baptized into one body, whether Jews or Greeks, whether bond or free; and were ALL made to drink of one Spirit" —I Corinthians 12:13 ASV.

(Note that the First Corinthian Epistle was written to "all that in every place call upon the Name of Jesus Christ our Lord—1:1-2)

10. **Prove that since Pentecost all true believers are indwelt by the Holy Spirit.**

"Know ye not that your body is the temple of the Holy Spirit which is in you, which ye have of God, and ye are not your own"—I Corinthians 6:19.

(John 14:17; Acts 10:47; Rom. 8:9; Gal. 3:2; 4:6; II Tim. 1:14

11. What other special works does the Holy Spirit accomplish in and for the true Christian?

"But the Comforter, which is the Holy Spirit, whom the Father will send in My Name, He shall TEACH YOU all things, and bring all things to your remembrance, whatsoever I have said unto you"—John 14:26.

(Acts 1:8; 9:31; 13:2-4; Rom. 5:5; 8:11, 16, 26; 15:13; Gal. 5:22-23; Eph. 3:16; II Thess. 2:13)

12. What does the Bible teach about the gifts bestowed upon us by the Holy Spirit?

"Now there are diversities of gifts, but the same Spirit . . . But all these worketh that one and the selfsame Spirit, dividing to every man severally as He will"—I Corinthians 12:4, 11.

(Born. 12:6-8; I Cor. 12:4-11, 27-31; I Pet. 4:10-11)

13. What does the Bible teach about the infilling of the Holy Spirit?

"Be not drunk with wine, wherein is excess; but be filled with the Spirit"—Ephesians 5:18.

(Acts 4:31; 6:1-3; 7:55-60; 9:17; 11:24)

14. What are some wrong attitudes toward the Holy Spirit?

"And GRIEVE NOT the Holy Spirit of God, whereby ye are sealed unto the day of redemption"—Ephesians 4:30.

(I Thess. 5:19) (The following passages refer to unbelievers: Mark 3:28-29; Acts 7:51; 8:18-22; Heb. 10:29)

15. What are some of the right attitudes we should take toward the Holy Spirit?

"If we live in the Spirit, let us also walk in the Spirit"—Galatians 5:25.

(Rom. 8:14; Gal. 5:16; Eph. 4:3; 6:18)

V. THE WORLD

1. **Was there ever a time when the world did not exist?**
   "Before the mountains were brought forth, or ever Thou hadst formed the earth and the world, even from everlasting to everlasting, Thou art God" —Psalm 90:2.
   (John 17:5, 24)

2. **When and how did the world begin?**
   In the beginning GOD CREATED the heaven and the earth"—Genesis 1:1.
   (Ps. 146:5-6; Isa. 42:5; 44:24; 45:12; Acts 14:15)

3. **How did God create the world?**
   "By the WORD of the Lord were the heavens made . . . For He spake, and it was done; He commanded, and it stood fast"—Psalm 33:6, 9.
   (Ps. 148:5; Jer. 10:12; Eph. 3:9; Heb. 11:3)

4. **What part did our Lord Jesus Christ have in creating the world?**
   "All things were made by Him; and without Him was not anything made that was made"—John 1:3.
   (John 1:10; I Cor. 8:6; Heb. 1:2)

5. **What part did the Holy Spirit have in the creation of the world?**
   "By His Spirit He hath garnished [beautified] the heavens"—Job 26:13.
   (Ps. 104:27-30)

6. **What does the Bible teach about the creation of the animal and plant life?**
   "And God made the beast of the earth AFTER HIS KIND, and cattle AFTER THEIR KIND, and everything that creepeth upon the earth AFTER HIS KIND; and God saw that it was good"—Genesis 1:25.
   (Gen. 1:11-12. 20-24; 2:19-20)

7. What does the Bible teach about the creation of man?

"So God created man IN HIS OWN IMAGE; in the image of God created He him; male and female created He them"—Genesis 1:27.

(Gen. 1:26, 28-30; 2:7, 20-24)

8. What work does God keep on doing in the world after creating it?

"Thou, even Thou, art Lord alone; Thou hast made heaven, the heaven of heavens, with all their host, the earth, and all things that are therein, the seas, and all that is therein, and THOU PRESERVEST THEM ALL"—Nehemiah 9:6.

(Psa. 36:6; 66:9; John 5:17; Acts 17:28; Col. 1:17 ASV margin)

9. Why did God create the world?

"Thou art worthy, O Lord, to receive glory and honour and power; for Thou hast created all things, and FOR THY PLEASURE they are and were created"—Revelation 4:11.

(Isa. 43:7; Col. 1:16 last phrase)

10. Was there any sin or imperfection in the world as God created it?

"And God saw everything that He had made, and, behold, it was VERY GOOD"—Genesis 1:31.

(Deut. 32:4a; Isa. 45:18 ASV)

11. How did sin, imperfection and death enter the world?

"BY ONE MAN sin entered into the world, and death by sin; and so death passed upon all men, for that all have sinned"—Romans 5:12.

(Gen. 2:16-17 with 3:6; Rom. 5:15-17; 8:20-22; I Cor. 15:21)

12. Will this world continue forever in its present imperfect condition?

"But the heavens and the earth, which are now, by the same word are kept in store, reserved unto fire against the Day of Judgment and perdition of ungodly men"—II Peter 3:7.

(I Cor. 15:24-26; Heb. 12:26-27; II Pet. 3:10)

13. What are we taught to look for after the destruction of this present evil world?

"Nevertheless we, according to His promise, look for NEW heavens and a NEW earth, wherein dwelleth righteousness"—II Peter 3:13.

(Isa. 66:22; Rev. 21:1, 5)

14. What should we learn from seeing the wonderful works of God?

"O Lord, Thou art my God; I will exalt Thee, I will praise Thy Name; for Thou hast done wonderful things"—Isaiah 25:1.

(Psa. 104:24; 111:2; 139:14; 145:4-5, 9-10, 17)

NOTES

VI. ANGELS

1. **What kind of beings are the angels?**

   "Are they not all ministering SPIRITS, sent forth to minister for them who shall be heirs of salvation" —Hebrews 1:14.

   (Ps. 148:2 with 5; Matt. 28:2-4; Mark 12:25; Luke 20:36a; Rev. 18:1)

2. **What are some other names given to angels in the Bible?**

   "This matter is by the decree of the WATCHERS, and the demand by the word of the HOLY ONES; to the intent that the living may know that the Most High ruleth in the kingdom of men"—Daniel 4:17a.

   (Gen. 32:1-2; Job 1:6; Ps. 89:6; Luke 24:4; Eph. 3:10)

3. **How many angels are there?**

   "And I beheld, and I heard the voice of many angels round about the throne . . . and the number of them was ten thousand times ten thousand, and thousands of thousands"—Revelation 5:11.

   (Dan. 710 Heb. 12:22)

4. **What does the Bible teach about the power of angels?**

   "Bless the Lord, ye His angels, that EXCEL in STRENGTH, that do His commandments, hearkening unto the voice of His Word"—Psalm 103:20.

   (Dan. 9:21; Matt. 28:2 with Mark 16:4; Acts 12:7, 23; II Pet. 2:11; Rev. 7:1)

5. **What two kinds of angels are there?**

   "The holy angels"—Mark 8:38. "The angels that sinned"—II Peter 2:4.

6. **What work in relation to Christ is done by good angels?**

   "And the angel said unto them, Fear not; for, behold, I bring you good tidings of great joy, which shall be to all people. For unto you is born this day in the city of David a Saviour, which is Christ the Lord"—Luke 2:10-11.

   (Matt. 2:13; 4:11; 28:5-6; Luke 22:43; Acts 1:10-11; Rev. 5:11-12)

7. **What work in relation to God's people is done by good angels?**

"For He shall give His angels charge over thee, to keep thee in all thy ways. They shall bear thee up in their hands, lest thou dash thy foot against a stone"—Psalm 91:11-12.

(Matt. 18:10; 24:31; Luke 16:22; Acts 12:5-7; 27:23-24; 5: 19-20; Heb 1:14)

8. **What work in relation to the wicked is done by good angels?**

"The Son of Man shall send forth His angels, and they shall gather out of His kingdom all things that offend, and them which do iniquity; and shall cast them into a furnace of fire"—Matthew 13:4142.

(Matt. 13:49-50; Acts 12:23; Rev. 16:1; 20:1-3)

NOTES

VII. SATAN

1. **What names are applied to the greatest of all evil spirits?**

   "The great DRAGON . . . that old SERPENT, called the DEVIL, and SATAN, which deceiveth the whole world"—Revelation 12:9.

   (Matt. 4:3; I John 2:14; Rev. 12:10)

2. **What was Satan like when God created him?**

   "Thus saith the Lord God; Thou sealest up the sum, full of wisdom, and perfect in beauty . . . Thou wast PERFECT IN THY WAYS from the day that thou was created, till iniquity was found in thee"—Ezekiel 28:12b, 15.

   (Ezek. 28:13-14)

3. **How did Satan become an evil spirit?**

   "Thine heart was lifted up because of thy beauty, thou hast corrupted thy wisdom by reason of thy brightness"—Ezekiel 28:17a.

   (Isa. 14:13-14; I Tim. 3:7)

4. **What is the present character of Satan?**

   "He was a MURDERER from the beginning, and abode not in the truth, because there is no truth in him. When he speaketh a lie, he speaketh of his own; for he is a LIAR, and the father of it"—John 8:44.

   (I John 3:8)

5. **How much liberty does God permit Satan to have at present?**

   "Now there was a day when the sons of God came to present themselves BEFORE THE LORD, and Satan came also among them. And the Lord said unto Satan, Whence comest thou? Then Satan answered the Lord, and said, From going to and fro IN THE EARTH, and from walking up and down in it"—Job 1:6-7.

   (Zech. 3:1-2; Eph. 2:2; I Pet. 5:8)

6. What are some of the powers of Satan?

"The working of Satan with all power and signs and lying wonders"—II Thessalonians 2:9.

(Job 1:7-19; Luke 13:11 with 16; 22:3; John 13:2; Acts 5:3; 10:38; Heb. 2:14)

7. Prove that Satan is the leader of other evil angels and spirits.

"And Satan, which deceiveth the whole world: he was cast out into the earth, and HIS ANGELS were cast out with him"—Revelation 12:9b.

(Matt. 25:41; 12:24-26

8. What position does Satan hold in the world of evil men?

"The GOD OF THIS WORLD hath blinded the minds of them which believe not, lest the light of the glorious gospel of Christ, Who is the image of God, should shine unto them"—II Corinthians 4:4.

(John 8:44a; 14:30; I John 5:19 ASV)

9. How does Satan seek to hinder the work of God?

"The field is the world; the good seed are the children of the Kingdom; but the tares are the children of the Wicked One; the enemy that sowed them is the Devil"—Matthew 13:38-39a.

(Gen. 3:1-6; Matt. 16:21-23: Luke 4:1-2; II Cor. 11:14-15)

10. How does Satan seek to injure the people of God?

"Be sober, be vigilant; because your adversary the Devil, as a roaring lion, walketh about, seeking whom he may devour"—I Peter 5:8.

(I Thess. 2:18; I Tim. 3:7; Rev. 2:10; 12:10)

11. How does Satan work against unsaved men and nations?

"The seed is the Word of God . . . Then cometh the Devil, and taketh away the Word out of their hearts, lest they should believe and be saved"—Luke 8:11-12.

(Acts 5:3; II Cor. 4:4; I John 3:12; Rev. 20:3)

12. Prove that Christ came to judge and destroy Satan and his works.

"He that committeth sin is of the Devil, for the Devil sinneth from the beginning. For this purpose the Son of God was manifested, that He might destroy the works of the Devil"—I John 3:8.

(John 12:31-32; 16:7-11; Heb. 2:14)

13. What will be the final doom of Satan and his followers?

"Then shall He say also unto them on the left hand, Depart from Me, ye cursed, into everlasting fire, prepared for the Devil and his angels"—Matthew 25:41.

(Rev. 12:7-9, 12; 20:1-3, 7-10)

14. How can we always win the battle against Satan?

"Finally, my brethren, be strong IN THE LORD, and in the power of HIS MIGHT. Put on the WHOLE ARMOUR OF GOD, that ye may be able to stand against the wiles of the Devil"—Ephesians 6:10-11.

(Eph. 4:27; 6:12-18; James 4:7; Rev. 12:11)

NOTES

VIII. SIN

1. What is sin, according to the Bible?

"Sin is the transgression of the law"—I John 3:4.
"All unrighteousness is sin"—I John 5:17.

(Ps. 39:1; Prov. 14:21; 24:9; James 4:17; I John 3:15)

2. How many of us have sinned?

"ALL have sinned, and come short of the glory of God"—Romans 3:23.

(Ps. 143:2; Eccl. 7:20; Rom. 3:9-10; I John 1:8, 10)

3. Where does sin begin in each one of us?

"For from within, OUT OF THE HEART of men, proceed evil thoughts, adulteries, fornications, murders, thefts, covetousness, wickedness, deceit, lasciviousness, an evil eye, blasphemy, pride, foolishness: all these evil things come from WITHIN and defile the man"—Mark 7:21-23.

(Jer. 7:24; 17:9; Matt. 5:28; 15:18-19; Luke 11:39; Acts 8: 21-22)

4. How did sin begin in the human race?

"By one man sin entered into the world, and death by sin; and so death passed upon all men, for that all have sinned"—Romans 5:12.

(Gen. 2:16-17 with 3:6)

5. What is at the bottom of all sin?

"He that speaketh of himself SEEKETH HIS OWN GLORY; but he that seeketh His glory that sent him, the same is true, and no unrighteousness is in him"—John 7:18.

(Cf. Matt. 22:36-38 with II Tim. 3:2a)

6. Against whom is all sin committed?

"Behold, ye have sinned AGAINST THE LORD; and be sure your sin will find you out"—Numbers 32:23.

(I Sam. 12:23; Prov. 8:36; I Cor. 8:12)

7. What is God's attitude toward sin?

"For thou art not a God that hath pleasure in wicked-

ness; neither shall evil dwell with Thee . . . Thou
HATEST all workers of iniquity"—Psalm 5:4-5.
(Psa. 34:16; 45:7; 145:20; Prov. 6:16-19; Zech. 8:17)

8. Is it possible for us to hide our sins from God?

"O God, thou knowest my foolishness; and my sins
are not hid from Thee"—Psalm 69:5.
(Job 14:16; Ps. 139:1-4; Amos 5:12; Heb. 4:12-13)

9. What is the present result of sin?

"Your iniquities have separated between you and
your God, and your sins have hid His face from you,
that He will not hear"—Isaiah 59:2.
(Prov. 5:22; Isa. 57:20-21; John 8:34; Rom. 7:23; Eph. 2:1; 4:18-19;
Heb. 3:13)

10. What will be the final result of sin?

"When lust hath conceived, it bringeth forth sin; and
sin, when it is finished, bringeth forth DEATH"
—James 1:15.
(Matt. 13:40-42; Rom. 6:23; Rev. 21:8)

11. Does the amount of sin we commit make any difference in our guilt?

"For whosoever shall keep the whole law, and yet
offend in ONE point, he is GUILTY OF ALL"
—James 2:10.
(Rom. 3:19)

12. Prove that not to believe on Christ is the greatest of all sins.

"He that believeth not IS CONDEMNED ALREADY,
because he hath not believed in the Name of the only
begotten Son of God"—John 3:18.
(John 3:36; 16:8-9; Heb. 10:26-29)

IX. SALVATION

1. **Can we save ourselves from sin?**
   "By grace are ye saved through faith; and that NOT OF YOURSELVES; it is the gift of God"—Ephesians 2:8.
   (Matt. 19:25-26; Rom. 7:18; 8:7-8; II Pet. 2:14)

2. **Who is able to save us from sin?**
   "This is a faithful saying, and worthy of all acceptation, that CHRIST JESUS came into the world to have sinners; of whom I am chief"—I Timothy 1:15.
   (Matt. 1:21; Luke 2:11; John 1:29; 3:17; Heb. 7:25; I John 3:5)

3. **Is it possible to be saved apart from the Lord Jesus Christ?**
   "Neither is there salvation in any other: for THERE IS NONE OTHER name under heaven given among men, whereby we must be saved"—Acts 4:12.
   (Matt. 17:5-8; John 14:6; Heb. 2:1-3)

4. **What did Jesus Christ do to save sinners?**
   "But God commendeth His love toward us, in that, while we were yet sinners, CHRIST DIED FOR US"—Romans 5:8.
   (Matt. 20:28; Rom. 5:6; I Cor. 15:3; Gal. 1:4)

5. **Prove that Christ died in our stead, suffering the punishment that we deserved.**
   "But He was wounded for OUR transgressions, He was bruised for OUR iniquities; the chastisement of our peace was upon Him; and with His stripes we are healed. All we like sheep have gone astray; we have turned every one to his own way; and the Lord hath LAID ON HIM THE INIQUITY OF US ALL"—Isaiah 53:5-6.
   (II Cor. 5:19, 21; Gal. 3:13; I Pet. 2:24; 3:13)

6. **What must we do to be saved?**
   "BELIEVE on the Lord Jesus Christ, and thou shalt be saved"—Acts 16:31.
   (John 1:12; 3:14-16; 6:28-29, 40, 47; 20:30-31; Rom. 10: 9-11)

7. **Do any good works of ours help us to be saved?**
   "NOT BY WORKS of righteousness which we have done, but according to His mercy He saved us, by the washing of regeneration, and renewing of the Holy Spirit"—Titus 3:5.
   (Rom. 3:20; 4:4-5; Gal. 3:10)

8. **What does God do with our sins when we are saved?**
   "He hath not dealt with us after our sins; nor rewarded us according to our iniquities . . . As far as the east is from the west, so far hath HE REMOVED our transgressions from us"—Psalm 103: 10, 12.
   (Ps. 32:1; Isa. 43:25; Mic. 7:19; Rom. 4:6-7)

9. **What kind of life does God give to us who believe?**
   "And this is the record, that God hath given to us ETERNAL LIFE, and this life is in His Son. He that hath the Son hath life; and he that hath not the Son of God hath not life"—I John 5:11-12.
   (John 17:2-3; Rom. 6:23; I Tim. 1:16)

10. **Can those who have the gift of eternal life ever lose it?**
    "My sheep hear My voice, and I know them, and they follow Me; and I give unto them eternal life; and THEY SHALL NEVER PERISH, neither shall any man pluck them out of My hand"—John 10:27-28.
    (John 17:2 with 6:39; Rom. 11:29; Eph. 4:30; I Thess. 5:23-24)

11. **Can those who are saved ever be condemned?**
    "Verily, verily, I say unto you, He that heareth My word, and believeth on Him that sent Me, hath everlasting life, and SHALL NOT COME INTO CONDEMNATION; but is passed from death unto life"—John 5:24.
    (Rom. 8:1 ASV; 8:31-34, 38-39)

12. Is it possible for us to KNOW that we are saved forever?

"These things have I written unto you that believe on the Name of the Son of God; THAT YE MAY KNOW THAT YE HAVE ETERNAL LIFE"—I John 5:13.

(Rom. 8:28; Phil. 1:6; II Tim. 1:12)

13. If we are truly saved, how should we act?

"WE LOVE HIM, because He first loved us"—I John 4:19. "This is the love of God, that we KEEP HIS COMMANDMENTS"—I John 5:3.

(Eph. 2:10; 4:1; Col. 3:1-2; Titus 3:8; II Pet. 1:5-7 ASV; I John 3:10, 14-15)

14. If we are truly saved, what should be our attitude toward sin?

"I ACKNOWLEDGED my sin unto Thee, and mine iniquity have I NOT HID. I said, I will CONFESS my transgressions unto the Lord; and Thou forgavest the iniquity of my sin"—Psalm 32:5.

(Ps. 34:14; 119:11; 139:23-24; Prov. 8:13; 28:13; II Tim. 2:19)

15. By what names does the Bible call those who are saved?

"For One is your Master, even Christ; and all ye are BRETHREN"—Matthew 23:8.

("Brethren" over 200 times in the N. T.) (John 10:15; 13:16; 15:15; Acts 6:7; 11:26; Phil. 4:21)

X. SPIRITUAL BLESSINGS

1. **How many spiritual blessings has God bestowed upon those who are saved in Christ?**

   "Blessed be the God and Father of our Lord Jesus Christ, Who bath blessed us with ALL SPIRITUAL BLESSINGS in heavenly places in Christ"—Ephesians 1:3.

   (Rom. 8:32: II Cor. 8:9; II Pet. 1:3)

2. **What does the Bible teach about the blessing of our Election?**

   "He hath CHOSEN US in Him before the foundation of the world, that we should be holy and without blame before Him in love"—Ephesians 1:4.

   (John 15:16; Eph. 1:11; II Thess. 2:13; I Pet. 1:2)

3. **What does the Bible teach about the blessing of our Calling?**

   "Who hath saved us, and CALLED US with an holy calling, not according to our works, but according to His own purpose and grace, which was given us in Christ Jesus before the world began"—II Timothy 1:9.

   (Rom. 8:28; I Cor. 1:9; I Thess. 2:12; II Thess 214; Rev. 17:14)

4. **What does the Bible teach about the blessing of our Union with Christ?**

   "For no man ever yet hated his own flesh; but nourisheth and cherisheth it, even as the Lord the Church: for WE ARE MEMBERS OF HIS BODY" —Ephesians 5:29-30.

   (John 15:5; Rorn. 7:4 ASV; I Cor. 6:17)

5. **What does the Bible teach about the blessing of our Identification with Christ?**

   "I am CRUCIFIED WITH CHRIST: nevertheless I live; yet not I, but Christ liveth in me: and the life which I now live in the flesh I live by the faith of the

34

Son of God, Who loved me, and gave Himself for me"—Galatians 2:20.

(Rom. 6:4a; Eph. 2:5 ASV. 6; Col. 2:20; 3:1)

6. **What does the Bible teach about the blessing of our Position in Christ?**

"For in Him dwelleth all the fulness of the Godhead bodily: And ye are COMPLETE IN HIM" —Colossians 2:9-10.

(Rom. 8:1 ASV; Gal. 3:28; Eph. 1:13; I John 5:20)

7. **What does the Bible teach about the blessing of our Justification in Christ?**

"Being JUSTIFIED FREELY by His grace through the redemption that is in Christ Jesus"—Romans 3:24.

("'Justify" means "to declare and treat one as righteous"—Rom. 3:28; 4:2-5; 5:1; Gal. 2:16; Titus 3:7)

8. **What does the Bible teach about the, blessing of our Regeneration in Christ?**

"But as many as received Him, to them gave He the right to become CHILDREN OF GOD, even to them that believe on His name; WHO WERE BORN, not of blood, nor of the will of the flesh, nor of the will of man, but OF GOD"—John 1:12-13 ASV.

(John 3:3; II Cor. 5:17; I Pet. 1:23; I John 5:1, 18)

9. **What does the Bible teach about the blessing of our Adoption in Christ?**

"But when the fulness of the time was come, God sent forth His Son, made of a woman, made under the law, to redeem them that were under the law, that we might receive THE ADOPTION OF SONS" —Galatians 4:4-5.

("Adoption" means to "place legally as a son"—Rom. 8:15, 23; Gal. 3:26 ASV; 4:6; Eph. 1:5 ASV)

10. **What does the Bible teach about the blessing of our Sanctification which is past?**

"By the which we HAVE BEEN SANCTIFIED

through the offering of the Body of Jesus Christ: ONCE FOR ALL"—Hebrews 10:10 ASV.

("Sanctify" means to "set apart" from sin unto God I Con 1:2 30; 6:11; Heb. 10:14; 13:12)

11. What does the Bible teach about the blessing of our Sanctification which is present?

"Christ loved the Church, and gave Himself for it; That He might SANCTIFY and cleanse it with the washing of water BY THE WORD"—Ephesians 5:25-26.

(Ps. 119:9; John 15:3; 17:17; II Cor. 3:18)

12. What does the Bible teach about the blessing of our Sanctification which is future?

"And the God of peace Himself SANCTIFY YOU WHOLLY; and may your spirit and soul and body be preserved entire without blame AT THE COMING OF OUR LORD JESUS CHRIST"—I Thessalonians 5:23 ASV.

(I Thess. 3:12-13; I John 3:2)

13. What does the Bible teach about the blessing of our Victory in Christ?

"But thanks be to God, which GIVETH US THE VICTORY through our Lord Jesus Christ"—I Corinthians 15:57.

(John 16:33; I John 5:4-5; Rev. 12:11)

14. What does the Bible teach about the blessing of our Glorification in Christ?

"For I reckon that the sufferings of this present time are not worthy to be compared with THE GLORY WHICH SHALL BE REVEALED IN US"—Romans 8:18.

(John 17:22; Rom. 8:30; Col. 3:4; II Thess. 2:14; I Pet. 1:8)

15. How should we feel toward God for His numberless blessings?

"I will extol Thee, my God, O King; and I will bless Thy Name for ever and ever. Every day will I bless Thee; and I will praise Thy Name for ever and ever"—Psalm 145:1-2.

(Ps. 150:1-6)

XI. GENERAL CHRISTIAN DUTIES

1. **What has God given us to correct and instruct us in the way of righteousness?**

   "All Scripture is given by inspiration of God, and is profitable for doctrine, for reproof, for correction, for INSTRUCTION IN RIGHTEOUSNESS; that the man of God may be perfect, throughly furnished unto all good works"—II Timothy 3:16-17.

   (Ps. 119:35, 104-105, 130, 133; Matt. 22:29)

2. **What is the first duty of the new-born Christian?**

   "I beseech you therefore, brethren, by the mercies of God, that ye PRESENT YOUR BODIES a living sacrifice, holy, acceptable unto God, which is your reasonable service"—Romans 12: 1.

   (Matt. 16:24; Rom. 6:13, 16; I Cor. 6:20; Phil. 1:20-21)

3. **What does the Bible teach about our Walk as Christians?**

   "That ye might WALK WORTHY OF THE LORD unto all pleasing, being fruitful in every good work, and increasing in the knowledge of God" —Colossians 1:10.

   (Rom. 8:4; Gal. 5:16; Eph. 4:1, 17; 5:15-16; Phil. 3:17-18; I John 1:6)

4. **What does the Bible teach us about doing good?**

   "As we have therefore opportunity, let us DO GOOD UNTO ALL MEN, especially unto them who are of the household of faith"—Galatians 6:10.

   (Matt. 5:16; 7:17-18; II Cor. 9:8; Eph. 6:8; Titus 3:1, 8; Heb. 10:24; 13:20-21)

5. **What does the Bible teach us about showing Kindness and Mercy?**

   "And BE YE KIND one to another, tender-hearted, forgiving one another, even as God for Christ's sake hath forgiven you"—Ephesians 4:32.

   (Prov. 11:17; Matt. 5:7; Luke 6:36-37; Rom. 12:10; Col. 3:12 ASV; James 3:17)

6. **What does the Bible teach us about speaking the Truth?**
"Wherefore putting away lying, SPEAK EVERY MAN TRUTH with his neighbour; for we are members one of another"—Ephesians 4:25.
(Exod. 18:21; Ps. 141:3; Prov. 12:22; I John 2:21; Rev. 21:8)

7. **What does the Bible teach us about being Honest?**
"And to work with your own hands, as we commanded you; that ye may WALK HONESTLY toward them that are without, and that ye may have lack of nothing"—I Thessalonians 4:11-12.
(Lev. 19:35-36; Deut. 25:13-16; Prov. 11:1; Mal. 3:5: Luke 16:11-12; Eph. 4:28)

8. **What does the Bible teach us about Moral Conduct?**
"Be not deceived: neither fornicators, nor idolaters, nor adulterers, nor effeminate, nor abusers of themselves with mankind, nor thieves, nor covetous, nor drunkards, nor revilers, nor extortioners, shall inherit the Kingdom of God"—I Corinthians 6:9-10.
(Prov. 6:32; Rom. 1:28-32; 13:9; I Cor. 6:18; Gal. 5:19-21; Col. 3:56; II Tim. 2:22)

9. **What does the Bible teach us about our Conversation?**
"Let NO CORRUPT COMMUNICATION proceed out of your mouth, but that which is good to the use of edifying, that it may minister grace unto the hearers"—Ephesians 4:29.
(Ps. 119:27; Prov. 21:23; Matt. 12:36-37; Eph. 5:3-4; James 1:26; 3:1-12; II Pet. 2:6-7)

10. **What does the Bible teach us about our Thoughts?**
"Finally, brethren, whatsoever things are true, whatsoever things are honest, whatsoever things are just, whatsoever things are pure, whatsoever things are lovely, whatsoever things are of good report; if there be any virtue, and if there be any praise, THINK ON THESE THINGS"—Philippians 4:8.
(Ps. 19:14; Prov. 23:7; 24:9; Matt. 5:27-28; I Cor. 13:5; II Cor. 10:5)

XII. CHRISTIAN WORSHIP AND WORK

1. **What does the Bible teach us about attending the Meetings of the Church?**

   "NOT FORSAKING THE ASSEMBLING OF OUR-SELVES TOGETHER, as the manner of some is; but exhorting one another: and so much the more, as ye see the Day approaching"—Hebrews 10:25.

   (Ps. 122:1; Luke 4:16; Acts 11:26; 14:27; 20:7; I Tim. 3:14-15)

2. **What does the Bible teach us about Worship?**

   "Thou shalt WORSHIP THE LORD THY GOD, and Him only shalt thou serve"—Luke 4:8.

   (Psa. 29:2; 95:6; 99:5, 9; Hab. 2:20; John 4:24)

3. **What does the Bible teach us about Prayer?**

   "In everything by prayer and supplication with thanksgiving LET YOUR REQUESTS BE MADE KNOWN UNTO GOD: And the peace of God, which passeth all understanding, shall keep your hearts and minds through Christ Jesus"—Philippians 4:6-7.

   (John 14:13-14; 16:23-24; Rom. 8:26; Eph. 6:18; I Thess. 5:17; I John 5:14)

4. **What does the Bible teach us about the study of God's Word?**

   "STUDY to show thyself approved unto God, a workman that needeth not to be ashamed, rightly dividing the Word of Truth"—II Timothy 2:15.

   (Deut 6:6-7; 17:19; Ps. 119:130; John 5:39; Acts 17:11; Rev. 1:3)

5. **What does the Bible teach us about singing Songs of Praise?**

   "Let the Word of Christ dwell in you richly in all wisdom; teaching and admonishing one another in PSALMS and HYMNS and SPIRITUAL SONGS, singing with grace in your hearts to the Lord"—Colossians 3:16.

   (I Chron. 15:16, 22; Psa. 33:2-3; 95:1-2; 104:33; Rev. 5:9)

6. **What does the Bible teach us about Giving to the Lord?**

"Every man according as he purposeth in his heart, so let him give; not grudgingly, or of necessity; for GOD LOVETH A CHEERFUL GIVER" —II Corinthians 9:7.

(Mal. 3:8-10; Matt. 6:1-4; Mark 12:41-44; Acts 20:35; I Cor. 9: 13-14; 16:1-2; II Cor. 9:6; Heb. 7:1-2)

7. **What does the Bible teach about our Testimony in word and life?**

"And they overcame him by the Blood of the Lamb, and by the WORD of their TESTIMONY" —Revelation 12:11.

(Psa. 107:1-2; 51:15; Ma!. 3:16; I Tim. 4:12; II Tim. 1:8)

8. **What does the Bible teach about winning others for Christ?**

"And Jesus said unto them, Come ye after Me, and I will make you to become FISHERS OF MEN" —Mark 1:17.

(Dan. 12:3; John 1:40-42; Acts 8:26-39; 20:20; 26:28; Rom. 1:16)

9. **What does the Bible teach us about Missionary Work?**

"How shall they believe in Him of whom they have not heard? And how shall they hear without a preacher? And how shall they preach, EXCEPT THEY BE SENT?"—Romans 10:14-15.

(Isa. 6:8; Mark 16:15; Acts 1:8; 8:4; II Cor. 5:19; III John 5-7)

10. **What does the Bible teach us about Unity in the Church?**

"That they ALL MAY BE ONE; as Thou Father, art in Me, and I in Thee, that they also may be ONE IN US: that the world may believe that Thou hast sent Me"—John 17:21.

(Rom. 16:17; I Cor. 1:10-13; 12:25-26; Gal. 3:28; Eph. 4:3-6; Phil. 2:1-4)

11. What does the Bible teach us about Difficulties between Christians?

"Moreover if thy brother shall trespass against thee, go and tell him his fault between thee and him alone; if he shall hear thee, thou hast gained thy brother. But if he will not hear thee, then take with thee one or two more, that in the mouth of two or three witnesses every word may be established. And if he shall neglect to hear them, tell it unto the church: but if he neglect to hear the church, let him be unto thee as an heathen man and a publican"—Matthew 18:15-17.

(Gal. 6:1; I Cor. 6:1-7; I Thess. 5:15)

12. What does the Bible teach about selling things in the House of God?

"And when He had made a scourge of small cords, He drove them all out of the temple . . . And said unto them that sold doves, TAKE THESE THINGS HENCE; make not My Father's House an house of merchandise"—John 2:15-16.

(II Sam. 24:24; Matt. 21:12-13; Mark 11:15-18; Luke 19:45-46)

NOTES

XIII. CHRISTIAN RELATIONSHIPS

1. **What does the Bible teach us about Marriage?**
   "For this cause shall a man leave his father and mother, and shall be joined unto his wife, and they two shall be one flesh"—Ephesians 5:31.
   (Gen. 2:18, 21-24; Prov. 18:22; 19:14; I Tim. 3:2, 12; 4:1-3; 5:14; Heb. 13:4)

2. **What does the Bible teach us about Divorce?**
   "What therefore God hath joined together, let not man put asunder"—Matthew 19:6.
   (Matt. 19:3-9; Rom. 7:1-3; I Cor. 7:10, 39)

3. **What does the Bible teach about the relation of Husbands and Wives?**
   "Therefore as the Church is subject unto Christ, so let the WIVES be to their own husbands in everything. HUSBANDS, love your wives, even as Christ also loved the Church, and gave Himself for it"—Ephesians 5:24-25.
   (Eph. 5:28, 33; Col. 3:18-19; I Pet. 3:1-2, 7)

4. **What does the Bible teach about the relation of Parents and Children?**
   "CHILDREN, obey your parents in all things: for this is well pleasing unto the Lord. FATHERS, provoke not your children to anger, lest they be discouraged"—Colossians 3:20-21.
   (Psa. 103:13; 127:3; II Cor. 12:14; Eph. 6:1-4; I Tim. 3:4, 12)

5. **What does the Bible teach about the relation of Masters and Servants?**
   "Servants, obey in all things your masters according to the flesh; not with eye-service, as men-pleasers; but in singleness of heart, fearing God . . . MASTERS, give unto your servants that which is just and equal; knowing that ye also have a Master in heaven"—Colossians 3:22; 4:1.
   (Eph. 6:5-9; Col. 3:22 to 4:1; Philem. 15-17; James 5:1-8)

6. What does the Bible teach about our obligation to the Weak?

"We that are strong ought to bear the infirmities of the weak, and not to please ourselves . . . For even Christ pleased not Himself"—Romans 15:1, 3.

(Rom. 14:1-23; I Cor. 8:9-13)

7. What does the Bible teach about our obligation to the Needy?

"But if any provide not for his own, and specially for those of his own house, he hath denied the faith, and is worse than an infidel"—I Timothy 5:8.

(Deut. 15:7-11; Prov. 19:17; Mark 14:7; Luke 14:13-14: Acts 2:45; 6:1-6; 11dm. 15:26; Gal. 2:10; James 2:1-5)

NOTES

XIV. CHRISTIAN ATTITUDES

1. **What does the Bible teach about our attitude toward the World?**

   "Love not the world, neither the things that are in the world. If any man love the world, the love of the Father is not in him"—I John 2:15.

   (Mark 8:36; John 17:14-16; Rom. 12:2; Gal. 6:14; James 1:27; 4:4; I John 2:17)

2. **What does the Bible teach about our attitude toward Government?**

   "Let every soul be subject unto the higher powers. For there is no power but of God: the powers that be are ordained of God"—Romans 13:1.

   (Dan. 4:17; Matt. 22:17-21; Acts 5:26-29); Rom. 13:3-7; Titus 3:1; I Pet. 2:13-17; II Pet. 2:10-11)

3. **What does the Bible teach about our attitude toward War?**

   "For though we walk in the flesh, we do not war after the flesh: for the weapons of our warfare are not carnal"—II Corinthians 10:3-4.

   (Matt. 26:52; Luke 9:51-56; John 18:36; Rom. 12:18-21; 13: 9-10; Eph. 6:12; Rev. 13:10; 20:7-8)

4. **What does the Bible teach about our attitude toward Enemies?**

   "LOVE your enemies, BLESS them that curse you, DO GOOD to them that hate you, and PRAY for them which despitefully use you, and persecute you"—Matthew 5:44.

   (Prov. 24:17; Luke 6:35; John 15:20; Rom. 12:20; II Cor. 12:10; II Tim. 3:12; I Pet. 2:19-23)

5. **What does the Bible teach about our attitude toward Money?**

   "For the love of money is a root of all kinds of evil: which some reaching after have been led astray from the faith, and have pierced themselves through with many sorrows"—I Timothy 6:10 ASV.

(Prov. 15:16; 22:1; 28:22; Matt. 6:19-21; 13:22; Luke 12: 13:21; I Tim. 6:6-9, 17-19; II Cor. 8:9)

6. What does the Bible teach about our attitude toward Worldly Habits?

"But put ye on the Lord Jesus Christ, and make not provision for the flesh, to fulfill the lusts thereof" —Romans 13:14.

(Jer. 13:23; John 8:34-36; I Cor. 3:17; II Cor. 7:1; Phil. 4:13; II Tim. 2:22; I Pet. 2:11; II Pet. 2:20-22)

7. What does the Bible teach about our attitude toward Worldly Pleasures?

"Choosing rather to suffer affliction with the people of God, than to enjoy the pleasures of sin for a season"—Hebrews 11:25.

(Ps. 16:11; Prov. 21:17; Eccl. 2:1; I Cor. 10:6-7; I Thess. 5:22; I Tim. 5:6; Titus 3:3)

8. What does the Bible teach about our attitude toward Worldly Companions?

"Blessed is the man that walketh not in the counsel of the ungodly, nor standeth in the way of sinners, nor sitteth in the seat of the scornful"—Psalm 1:1.

(Prov. 4:14-15; 13:20; I Cor. 15:33; II Cor. 6:14-18)

9. What does the Bible teach about our attitude toward Swearing?

"But above all things, my brethren, SWEAR NOT, neither by heaven, neither by the earth, NEITHER BY ANY OTHER OATH, but let your yea be yea; and your nay, nay: lest ye fall into condemnation" —James 5:12.

(Matt. 5:33-37)

XV. PRECIOUS PROMISES

1. **What kind of promises has God given to us who believe in Christ?**
   "Whereby are given unto us exceeding GREAT and PRECIOUS promises"—II Peter 1:4.
   (Rom. 4:16; II Cor. 1:20; Heb. 8:6)

2. **What has God promised about supplying our need?**
   "But my God shall supply ALL YOUR NEED according to His riches in glory by Christ Jesus"—Philippians 4:19.
   (Ps. 84:11; Matt. 6:8; Rom. 8:32)

3. **What has God promised about being with us?**
   "Lo, I am WITH YOU ALWAY, even unto the end of the world"—Matthew 28:20.
   (Matt. 18:20; Acts 18:10; Heb. 13:5-6)

4. **What has God promised about guiding us?**
   "Trust in the Lord with all thine heart; and lean not unto thine own understanding. In all thy ways acknowledge Him, and HE SHALL DIRECT THY PATHS"—Proverbs 3:5-6.
   (Psa. 23:3; 48:14; 73:24; Jer. 10:23; John 10:4)

5. **What has God promised about giving us wisdom?**
   "If any of you lack wisdom, let him ask of God, that giveth to all men liberally, and upbraideth not; and IT SHALL BE GIVEN HIM"—James 1:5.
   (Prov. 2:6; Luke 21:15; Col. 2:3; James 3:17)

6. **What has God promised about giving us strength?**
   "Fear thou not; for I am with thee: be not dismayed; for I am thy God: I WILL STRENGTHEN THEE; yea, I will uphold thee with the right hand of My righteousness"—Isaiah 41:10).
   (Eph. 3:16; Phil. 4:13; Col. 1:11; II Tim. 4:17)

7. What has God promised us about helping us in temptation?

"God is faithful, Who will not suffer you to be tempted above that ye are able; but will with the temptation also make a way to escape, that ye may be able to bear it"—I Corinthians 10:13.

(Matt. 4:1; Heb. 2:18; II Pet. 2:9)

8. What has God promised about forgiving our sins?

"If we confess our sins, He is faithful and just to forgive us our sins, and to cleanse us from all Unrighteousness"—I John 1:9.

(Ps. 86:5; Eph. 4:32)

9. What has God promised about answering our prayers?

"If ye then, being evil, know how to give good gifts unto your children, how much more shall your Father which is in heaven give good things to them that ask Him"—Matthew 7:11.

(Psa. 66:18-20; 91:15; 99:6; Matt. 21:22; John 14:13; I Pet. 3:12)

10. What has God promised about chastening us?

"My son, despise not thou the chastening of the Lord, nor faint when thou art rebuked of Him; for WHOM THE LORD LOVETH HE CHASTENETH, and scourgeth every son whom He receiveth" —Hebrews 12:5-6.

(Psa. 94:12; 119:67, 75; I Cor. 11:32; Heb. 12:5-11; Rev. 3: 19)

11. What has God promised about healing our bodies?

"Is any sick among you? Let him call for the elders of the church; and let them pray over him, anointing him with oil in the name of the Lord: and the prayer of faith shall save the sick, and the Lord shall raise him up"—James 5:14-15.

(Ps. 103:3; I John 5:14)

12. What has God promised, if it should not be His will to heal us?

"MY GRACE IS SUFFICIENT FOR THEE; for My

strength is made perfect in weakness. Most gladly therefore will I rather glory in my infirmities, that the power of Christ may rest upon me" —II Corinthians 12:9.

(II Cor. 12:7-10; Phil. 4:6-7)

13. What has God promised about giving us comfort in sorrow?

"Blessed be God, even the Father of our Lord Jesus Christ, the Father of mercies, and the God of all comfort; WHO COMFORTETH US in all our tribulation, that we may be able to comfort them which are in any trouble, by the comfort wherewith we ourselves are comforted of God"—II Corinthians 1:3-4.

(Matt. 5:4: John 14:16, 18; II Thess. 2:16-17)

14. What has God promised about giving us rest?

"Come unto Me, all ye that labor and are heavy laden, and I WILL GIVE YOU REST. Take My yoke upon you, and learn of Me; for I am meek and lowly in heart: and ye shall find rest unto your souls" — Matthew 11:28-29.

(Ps. 23:2; Isa. 57:20; Heb. 4:3, 9-10)

15. What has God promised about making all things work for our good?

"And we know that all things work together for good to them that love God, to them who are the called according to His purpose"—Romans 8:28.

(Rom. 8:37; I Cor. 3:21-23; II Cor. 2:14; Eph. 1:11)

16. What has God promised about preserving and delivering us?

"The Lord shall preserve thee from all evil: He shall preserve thy soul. The Lord shall preserve thy going out and thy coming in from this time forth, and even for evermore"—Psalm 121:7-8.

(Ps. 97:10; II Tim. 4:18; Jude 1)

17. Is God able to do all that He has promised for us?

"Now unto Him that is able to do exceeding abundantly above all that we ask or think, according to the power that worketh in us"—Ephesians 3:20.

(I Kings 8:56; Dan. 3:17; Isa. 14:24; Heb. 6:17-18)

18. What should we do with the promises of God?

"He staggered not at the promise of God through unbelief; but was strong in faith, giving glory to God; and being fully persuaded that, what He had promised, He was able also to perform" —Romans 4:20-21.

(Ps. 37:5; Matt. 9:29; Heb. 6:12; 11:6)

NOTES

XVI. THE GREAT COMMISSION

1. **What was the Great Threefold Commandment given by our Lord just before He ascended into heaven?**

   "All authority hath been given unto Me in heaven and on earth. Go ye therefore, and MAKE DISCIPLES of all the nations, BAPTIZING THEM into the name of the Father and of the Son and of the Holy Spirit; TEACHING THEM to observe all things whatsoever I commanded you: and lo, I am with you alway, even unto the end of the world"—Matthew 28:18-20 ASV.

2. **What does God the Father teach us about the authority of His Son?**

   "This is my beloved Son, in Whom I am well pleased; HEAR YE HIM"—Matthew 17:5.

3. **What does Christ Himself teach us about keeping His commandments?**

   "He that hath MY commandments, and keepeth them, he it is that loveth Me; and he that loveth Me shall be loved of My Father, and I will love him, and will manifest Myself to him"—John 14:21.

4. **What does the Apostle Paul say about those who refuse to obey the words of our Lord Jesus Christ?**

   "If any man teach otherwise, and consent not to wholesome words, even THE WORDS OF OUR LORD JESUS CHRIST . . . He is proud, knowing nothing . . . from such withdraw thyself"—I Timothy 6:3-5.

5. **What does the Apostle John teach about our keeping the commandments of Christ?**

   "And hereby we do know that we know Him, if we keep His commandments. He that saith, I know Him, and keepeth not His commandments, is a liar, and the truth is not in him"—I John 2:3-4.

XVII. THE GOSPEL

1. **What is the first and most important part of the Great Commission?**

   "Go ye therefore, and MAKE DISCIPLES of all the nations"—Matthew 28:19 ASV.

2. **What must we do to "make disciples"?**

   "GO ye into all the world, and PREACH THE GOSPEL to every creature"—Mark 16:15.

3. **What is this Gospel?**

   "Moreover, brethren, I declare unto you the Gospel which I preached unto you . . . For I delivered unto you first of all that which I also received, how that CHRIST DIED FOR OUR SINS according to the Scriptures; and that He was buried, and that HE ROSE AGAIN the third day according to the Scriptures"—I Corinthians 15:1-4.

4. **What does the Apostle Paul say about those who preach some other gospel?**

   "But though we, or an angel from heaven, preach any other Gospel unto you than that which we have preached unto you, LET HIM BE ACCURSED"—Galatians 1:8.

5. **What does the Gospel of Christ do for all who believe it?**

   "I am not ashamed of the Gospel of Christ; for it is THE POWER OF GOD UNTO SALVATION to every one that believeth . . . For therein is the righteousness of God revealed from faith to faith; as it is written, The just shall live by faith"—Romans 1:16-17.

6. **What will be the end of all who reject the Gospel of Christ?**

   "In flaming fire taking vengeance on them that know not God, and that obey not the Gospel of our Lord Jesus Christ; who shall be PUNISHED WITH EVER-

LASTING DESTRUCTION from the presence of the Lord"—II Thessalonians 1:8-9.

7. How should we feel our personal responsibility for taking the Gospel to all men?

"For necessity is laid upon me; yea, woe is unto me, if I preach not the Gospel"—I Corinthians 9:16. "So, as much as in me is, I am ready to preach the Gospel to you"—Romans 1:15.

NOTES

XVIII. BAPTISM

1. **What did our Lord command in the second part of His Great Commission?**

   "BAPTIZING THEM into the name of the Father and of the Son and of the Holy Spirit"—Matthew 28:19 ASV.

2. **What does Acts 8:12 teach that we must do before being baptized?**

   "WHEN THEY BELIEVED . . . they were baptized . . .

3. **What does Acts 8:38 teach as to the proper place for baptism?**

   "And they went down both INTO THE WATER, both Philip and the eunuch; and he baptized him."

4. **What does Romans 6:4 teach as to the proper mode of baptism?**

   "Therefore WE ARE BURIED with Him by baptism into death . . .

5. **What does Matthew 28:19 teach as to the number of times we should be buried beneath the water in baptism?**

   "Baptizing them into the name of the FATHER and of the SON and of the HOLY SPIRIT" ASV.

6. **What does Romans 6:3-4 teach as to the meaning of baptism?**

   "Know ye not, that so many of us as were baptized into Jesus Christ were BAPTIZED INTO HIS DEATH? Therefore we are buried with Him by baptism into death; that like as Christ was raised up from the dead by the glory of the Father, even so we also SHOULD WALK IN NEWNESS OF LIFE."

7. **What should we do as we come forth from the baptismal waters?**

"Likewise RECKON ye also yourselves to be DEAD INDEED UNTO SIN, but ALIVE UNTO GOD through Jesus Christ our Lord"_Romans 6:11.

NOTES

XIX. THE WASHING OF ONE ANOTHER'S FEET

1. **What did our Lord command in the third part of His Great Commission?**

   "TEACHING THEM to observe all things whatsoever I have commanded you"—Matthew 28:20.

2. **What did Christ command about the washing of one another's feet?**

   "If I then, your Lord and Master, have washed your feet; ye also OUGHT TO WASH ONE ANOTHER'S FEET. For I have given you an example, that ye should do as I have done to you"—John 13:14-15.

3. **How did Christ teach that His action was not merely the observance of an ordinary custom of His day?**

   "Jesus answered and said unto him, WHAT I do THOU KNOWEST NOT NOW; but thou shalt know hereafter"—John 13:7.

4. **How did Christ teach that the service of feet washing is not too humble for us to do?**

   "Verily, verily, I say unto you, the servant is not greater than his Lord"—John 13:1.6.

5. **What blessing did Christ promise for those who obey His command to wash one another's feet?**

   "If ye know these things, happy are ye if ye do them"—John 13:17.

6. **What great present Work of Christ is symbolized as our feet are being washed?**

   "Christ also loved the Church, and gave Himself for it; that He might SANCTIFY and CLEANSE IT with the WASHING OF WATER BY THE WORD"—Ephesians 5:25-26.

7. **What great Christian duty is taught as we wash the feet of others?**

   "Brethren, if a man be overtaken in a fault, ye which are spiritual, RESTORE SUCH AN ONE in the spirit of meekness; considering thyself, lest thou also be tempted. BEAR YE ONE ANOTHER'S BURDENS, and so fulfill the law of Christ"—Galatians 6:1-2.

8. **What prayer should be in every heart during the service of feet-washing?**

   "SEARCH ME, O God, and know my heart; try me, and know my thoughts: and SEE IF THERE BE ANY WICKED WAY IN ME, and lead me in the way everlasting"—Psalm 139:23-24.

NOTES

XX. THE COMMUNION

1. **What did the Lord command us about partaking of the Bread and the Cup?**

   "The Lord Jesus the same night in which He was betrayed TOOK BREAD; and when He had given thanks, He brake it, and said, Take, eat; this is My Body, which is broken for you: this do in remembrance of Me. After the same manner also He TOOK THE CUP, when He had supped, saying, This Cup is the new testament in My Blood: this do ye, as oft as ye drink it, in remembrance of Me" —I Corinthians 11:23-25.

2. **What past work of Christ is symbolized by the Bread and the Cup?**

   "For as often as ye eat this Bread, and drink this Cup, ye do show the LORD'S DEATH till He come" —I Corinthians 11:26.

3. **How does our eating and drinking symbolize the appropriation of Christ's life by faith?**

   "Except ye eat the flesh of the Son of Man, and drink His Blood, ye have no life in you. Whoso eateth My flesh, and drinketh My Blood, hath eternal life; and I will raise him up at the last day" —John 6:53-54.

4. **What should we remember as we partake of the Bread and the Cup?**

   "The Cup of blessing which we bless, is it not the communion of the Blood of Christ? The Bread which we break, is it not the communion of the Body of Christ?" —I Corinthians 10:16.

5. **How does the Bible warn us about partaking of the Communion unworthily?**

   "Wherefore whosoever shall eat this Bread, and drink this Cup of the Lord, UNWORTHILY, shall be

guilty of the Body and Blood of the Lord"
—I Corinthians 11:27.

6. **What should each of us do, especially during the feet-washing service, as we approach the Communion?**
"But let a man EXAMINE HIMSELF, and so let him eat of that Bread, and drink of that Cup"
—I Corinthians 11:28.

7. **How can we be cleansed from all sin and be made worthy to partake of the Bread and the Cup?**
"If we CONFESS OUR SINS, He is faithful and just to forgive us our sins, and to cleanse us from all unrighteousness"—I John 1:9.

NOTES

XXI. THE LORD'S SUPPER

1. **Upon what occasion did our Lord institute the Washing of Feet?**

   "He riseth from SUPPER . . . and began to wash the disciples' feet"—John 13:4-5.

2. **When did our Lord institute the Breaking of Bread?**

   "As THEY WERE EATING, Jesus took bread, and blessed it, and brake it"—Matthew 26:26.

3. **When did our Lord institute the Drinking of the Cup?**

   "Likewise also the Cup AFTER SUPPER"—Luke 22:20.

4. **What does the Bible call that feast which we keep, and which the early churches kept, in commemoration of our Lord's last supper?**

   "The Lord's Supper"—I Corinthians 11:20. "Your love-feasts"—Jude 1 2 ASV.

5. **How do we know that our Lord's last supper was not the Jewish Passover?**

   "Now BEFORE THE FEAST OF THE PASSOVER . . . and supper being ended . . . He riseth from supper"—John 13:1-4 (see also verse 29).

6. **What great Christian truth is taught by our sitting down together to eat the Love-feast?**

   "A new commandment I give unto you, THAT YE LOVE ONE ANOTHER; as I have loved you, that we also love one another. By this shall all men know that ye are My disciples, if ye have love one to another"—John 13:34-35.

7. **To what great heavenly feast do we look forward as we eat the Love-feast?**

   "Let us be glad and rejoice, and give honor to Him; for the marriage of the Lamb is come, and His wife hath made herself ready . . . Blessed are they which are called unto THE MARRIAGE SUPPER OF THE LAMB"—Revelation 19:7-9.

8. Since we are the Bride of Christ, what should be our prayer as we eat the Love-feast?
"Even so, COME, Lord Jesus"-Revelation 22:20.

NOTES

XXII. THE CHURCH

1. **What is the Greek word for "Church" and what does it mean?**

   "Ecclesia"—a called out people.

   (Rom. 9:24; II Thess. 2:14; I Pet. 5:10)

2. **What is our Lord's first prophecy of the Church?**

   "And Simon Peter answered and said, Thou are the Christ, the Son of the living God. And Jesus answered and said unto him . . . Upon this rock I WILL BUILD MY CHURCH; and the gates of hell shall not prevail against it"—Matthew 16:16-18.

3. **When did Christ begin the building of His Church?**

   "And when the DAY OF PENTECOST was fully come, they were all with one accord in one place . . . And the Lord added to the Church daily such as should be saved"—Acts 2:1, 47.

4. **What is the relation of the Church to Jesus Christ?**

   "And hath put all things under His feet, and gave Him to be the head over all things to the Church, WHICH IS HIS BODY, the fulness of Him that filleth all in all"—Ephesians 1:22-23.

   (Eph. 1:18; 2:21; I Pet. 5:2, 4; Rev. 19:7)

5. **What are the gifts by which our Lord builds up His church?**

   "And He gave some to be apostles; and some, prophets; and some, evangelists; and some, pastors and teachers; for the perfecting of the saints, unto the work of ministering, unto the BUILDING UP OF THE BODY OF CHRIST"—Ephesians 4:1112 ASV.

6. **What is God's great purpose in the Church?**

   "To the intent that now unto the principalities and powers in heavenly places might be known by the Church THE MANIFOLD WISDOM OF GOD, according to the eternal purpose which He purposed

61

in Christ Jesus our Lord"—Ephesians 3:10-11.
(Eph. 1:12; 2:7; I Pet. 2:9)

7. **How does the Holy Spirit make us members of the Church when we believe on Christ?**
"By one Spirit are we all baptized into one body, whether we be Jews or Gentiles, whether we be bond or free; and have been all made to drink into one Spirit"—I Corinthians 12:13.

8. **Are there any unsaved people in the true Church?**
"Now if any man have not the Spirit of Christ, he is none of His"—Romans 8:9.

9. **Is there more than one true Church?**
"There is ONE BODY, and ONE SPIRIT, even as ye are called in one hope of your calling; one Lord, one faith, one baptism, one God and Father of all, who is above all, and through all, and in you all"—Ephesians 4:4-6.
(I Cor. 12:12-13, 20; Eph. 2:16)

10. **Prove that the members of the one true Church associated themselves together in many local "churches."**
"And so were the CHURCHES established in the faith, and INCREASED in NUMBER daily"—Acts 16:5.
(Acts 14:23; Rom. 16:16; Gal. 1:2)

11. **Why did the early Christians form local churches?**
"And they continued stedfastly in the apostles' TEACHING and FELLOWSHIP, in the BREAKING OF BREAD and the PRAYERS"—Acts 2:42 ASV.

12. **What are the two offices in the local church?**
". . . the BISHOPS and DEACONS"—Philippians
("Bishop" and "elder" refer to the same office—Titus 1:5, 7)

13. **What are the qualifications of these two offices?**
"A BISHOP then must be blameless, the husband of one wife, vigilant, sober, of good behavior, given to

hospitality, apt to teach . . . Likewise must he DEA-
CONS be grave, not doubletongued, not given to much
wine, not greedy of filthy lucre"—I Timothy 3:2, 8.

(I Tim. 3:1-13; Titus 1:5-9)

14. May unsaved people sometimes enter the membership of the local church?

"But there were false prophets also among the people, even as there shall be FALSE TEACHERS
AMONG YOU, who privily shall bring in damnable
heresies, even denying the Lord that bought them,
and bring upon themselves swift destruction"
—II Peter 2:1.

(Acts 20:28-30; Gal. 2:4; Jude 4, 12)

15. How will the false at last be separated from the true members of the Church?

"The one shall be taken, and the other left. Watch
therefore; for ye know not what hour your Lord doth
come"—Matthew 24:41-42.

NOTES

XXIII. DEATH AND
THE INTERMEDIATE STATE

1. **How does the Bible describe Physical Death?**
   "The body without the spirit is dead"—James 2:26.
   (Gen. 35:18; Luke 23:46; I Cor. 15:26; II Pet. 3:4)

2. **What is the real cause of Death?**
   "Wherefore, as by one man sin entered into the world,
   and DEATH BY SIN; and so death passed upon all
   men, for that all have sinned"—Romans 5:12.
   (Gen. 2:17; 3:17-19; Ps. 90:7-11: James 1:14-15)

3. **Where do the spirits of the unsaved go when they die?**
   "The wicked shall be turned INTO HELL [Sheol],
   and all the nations that forget God"—Psalm 9:17.
   (Isa. 14:13-15; Matt. 11:20-23)

4. **What is the condition of the unsaved in hell?**
   "The rich man also died, and was buried; and in hell
   [Hades] he lift up his eyes, being IN TORMENTS"
   —Luke 16:22-23.
   (Deut. 32:22; Isa. 57:20-21; Luke 16:24-25, 28)

5. **Can anyone pass from hell to heaven after death?**
   "There is A GREAT GULF FIXED; so that they
   which would pass from hence to you cannot; neither
   can they pass to us, that would come from thence"
   —Luke 16:26.
   (Luke 16:22-26; John 8:21; II Pet. 2:4)

6. **Will all the unsaved die?**
   "It is appointed unto men once to die, but after this
   the judgment"—Hebrews 9:27.

7. **Where do all true believers go when they die?**
   "We are confident, I say, and willing rather to be
   absent from the body, and to be PRESENT WITH
   THE LORD"—II Corinthians 5:8.
   (Luke 23:43; Acts 7:55, 59-60; I Thess 5:10)

8. What is the condition of believers with Christ after death?

"For to me to live is Christ, and TO DIE IS GAIN . . . For I am in a strait betwixt two, having a desire to depart and to be with Christ; which is far better" — Philippians 1:21, 23.

(Heb. 12:22-23; Rev. 6:9-11; 7:13-17)

9. If we belong to Christ, do we need to fear Death?

"Yea, though I walk through the valley of the shadow of death, I WILL FEAR NO EVIL; for Thou art with me; Thy rod and Thy staff they comfort me" — Psalm 23:4.

(Rom. 8:38-39; I Cor. 15:56-57; Heb. 2:14-15)

10. Will all true believers pass through the sleep of death?

"Behold, I show you a mystery; WE SHALL NOT ALL SLEEP, but we shall all be changed" — I Corinthians 15:51.

(I Thess. 4:15; for further passages see next chapter)

NOTES

XXIV. THE SECOND COMING OF CHRIST

1. **Does the Old Testament teach that our Lord will return from heaven in judgment?**

   "Let the heavens rejoice, and let the earth be glad . . . before the Lord; FOR HE COMETH, for He cometh to judge the earth: He shall judge the world with righteousness, and the people with His truth" —Psalm 96:11-13.

   (Ps. 98:5-9; Isa. 40:9-11; Dan. 7:13-14; Zech. 14:3-4a)

2. **Did Christ Himself teach that He would come again?**

   "And if I go and prepare a place for you, I WILL COME AGAIN, and receive you unto Myself; that where I am, there ye may be also"—John 14:3.

   (Matt. 16:27; 26:63-64; Mark 8:38; Luke 21:27; Rev. 3:11)

3. **Do the New Testament writers teach that Christ will come again from heaven?**

   "For our citizenship is in heaven; whence also we wait for a Saviour, the Lord Jesus Christ"—Philippians 3:20 ASV.

   (Col. 3:4; James 5:7; I Pet. 5:4; I John 3:2; Jude 14)

4. **What did the angels declare about the second coming of Christ?**

   "This same Jesus, which is taken up from you into heaven, SHALL SO COME IN LIKE MANNER as ye have seen Him go into heaven"—Acts 1:11.

5. **How will Christ come at His second coming?**

   "And then shall they see the Son of Man coming in the clouds WITH GREAT POWER AND GLORY" —Mark 13:26.

   (Matt. 24:27; 25:31; Rev. 1:7. Contrast His first coming, Isa. 53:1-7)

6. **Does anyone know the time of Christ's second coming?**

   "But of that day and hour KNOWETH NO MAN, no,

not the angels of heaven, but My Father only"
—Matthew 24:36.

(Mark 13:32; Luke 12:40; Acts 1:7)

7. Should we look for Christ's coming at any moment?

"WATCH YE THEREFORE: for ye know not when
the Master of the house cometh, at even, or at mid-
night, or at the cock-crowing, or in the morning . . .
And what I say unto you I say unto all, WATCH"
—Mark 13:35, 37.

(Matt. 24:42-51; Phil. 3:20; I Thess. 1:10; Titus 2:12-13)

8. Will there be any signs which show that our Lord's coming is near at hand?

"And THERE SHALL BE SIGNS . . . And then shall
they see the Son of Man coming in a cloud with
power and great glory"—Luke 21:25, 27.

(Dan. 12:4; Matt. 24:24; Luke 17:26-30; 21:24-27; I Tim. 4:1-3;
II Tim. 3:1-5; James 5:1-7; II Pet. 3:1-4)

9. What will happen to Christ's people as He descends from heaven?

"For the Lord Himself shall descend from heaven
with a shout, with the voice of the archangel, and
with the trump of God; and the dead in Christ shall
rise first: then we which are alive and remain shall
BE CAUGHT up together with them in the clouds,
TO MEET THE LORD IN THE AIR; and so shall we
EVER BE WITH THE LORD"—I Thessalonians
4:16-17.

(John 14:2-3)

10. Will any true Christians be left behind on earth?

"WE SHALL ALL BE CHANGED, in a moment, in
the twinkling of an eye, at the last trump; for the
trumpet shall sound, and the dead shall be raised in-
corruptible, and we shall be changed"—I Corinthians
15:51-52.

(The above words were written to "all that in every place call upon the
name of Jesus Christ our Lord"—I Cor. 1:1-2)

11. What judgments will fall upon the world after Christ's people are taken up?

"Come, my people, enter thou into thy chambers, and shut thy doors about thee: hide thyself as it were for a little moment, until the indignation be overpast. For, behold, the Lord corneth out of His place TO PUNISH THE INHABITANTS OF THE EARTH FOR THEIR INIQUITY; the earth also shall disclose her blood, and shall no more cover her slain"—Isaiah 26:20-21.

(Isa 2:12-21; 24:1-6, 17-21; Matt. 24:21-22; Rev. 6:12-17. All the great judgments of Revelation, chapters 6 to 18, belong to this period of about seven years)

12. How will Christ come down to earth with His people after these terrible judgments?

"And I saw heaven opened, and behold a white horse; and He that sat upon him was called Faithful and True, and in righteousness He doth judge and make war . . . And THE ARMIES WHICH WERE IN HEAVEN FOLLOWED HIM upon white horses, clothed in fine linen, white and clean"—Revelation 19:11, 14.

(Col. 3:4; I Thess. 3:13; II Thess. 1:7-10)

13. What kind of a Kingdom will be given to our Lord when He comes to earth with His people?

"And, behold, one like the Son of Man came with the clouds of heaven, . . . And there was given him dominion, and glory, and a kingdom, that all people, nations, and languages, should serve Him: His dominion is an everlasting dominion, which shall not pass away, and His kingdom that which shall not be destroyed"—Daniel 7:13-14.

(Dan. 7:27; for other passages, see under "The Kingdom")

14. **Since our Lord may come for us at any moment, how should we live?**

"We should live soberly, righteously, and godly, in this present world; looking for that Blessed Hope, and the glorious appearing of the Great God and our Saviour Jesus Christ"—Titus 2:12-13.

15. **What shall be the reward for all who love Christ's coming?**

"A crown of righteousness, which the Lord, the righteous Judge, shall give me at that day; and not to me only, but unto all them also that LOVE HIS APPEARING"—II Timothy 4:8.

16. **If we really watch and hope for Christ's coming, how will our lives be made better?**

"And every man that hath this hope in Him PURIFI-ETH himself, even as He is pure"—I John 3:3.

NOTES

XXV. RESURRECTION AND REWARDS

(For Believers)

1. **Will the bodies of all people be sometime raised from the dead?**

   "For since by man came death, by man came also the resurrection of the dead. For as in Adam all die, even so in Christ shall ALL BE MADE ALIVE" —I Corinthians 15:21-22.
   (John 5:28)

2. **What two different Resurrections will there be?**

   "They that have done good, unto the RESURRECTION OF LIFE; and they that have done evil, unto the RESURRECTION OF DAMNATION"—John 5:29.
   (Acts 24:15)

3. **How much time will there be between these two Resurrections?**

   "And they lived and reigned with Christ a thousand years. But the rest of the dead lived not again until the THOUSAND YEARS were finished" —Revelation 20:4b-5a.
   (The "hour" of John 5:28 refers to a long period. Compare the "hour" in John 4:23 which has already lasted 1900 years)

4. **What names are applied to the Resurrection of Christ's people?**

   "This is THE FIRST RESURRECTION. Blessed and holy is he that hath part in the first resurrection"-Revelation 20:5b-6a.
   (Luke 14:14; 20:35; John 5:29b; Heb. 11:35)

5. **When will the First Resurrection begin?**

   "For THE LORD HIMSELF SHALL DESCEND from heaven with a shout, with the voice of the archangel, and with the trump of God; and THE DEAD IN CHRIST SHALL RISE FIRST" —I Thessalonians 4:16.

6. **What will happen to those Christians who are living when Christ comes?**

"Then we which are alive and remain shall BE CAUGHT UP TOGETHER WITH THEM in the clouds, to meet the Lord in the air; and so shall we ever be with the Lord"—I Thessalonians 4:17.

7. **How will the bodies of all believers be changed at the Coming of Christ?**

"The Lord Jesus Christ, Who shall FASHION ANEW THE BODY of our humiliation, that it may be CON-FORMED TO THE BODY OF HIS GLORY, according to the working whereby He is able even to subject all things unto Himself—Philippians 3:20-21 ASV.

(Rom. 8:11; I Cor. 15:51-54; I John 3:2)

8. **What was Christ's resurrection body like?**

"Behold My hands and My feet, that it is I Myself: handle Me, and see; for a spirit hath not flesh and bones, as ye see Me have"—Luke 24:39.

(Luke 24:34-43; John 20:19; Acts 1:9; Rev. 1:13-18)

9. **How does I Corinthians 15 describe our resurrection body?**

"It is sown in corruption; it is raised in INCOR-RUPTION: it is sown in dishonor; it is raised in GLORY: it is sown in weakness; it is raised in POWER: it is sown a natural body; it is raised a SPIRITUAL BODY"—I Corinthians 15:42-44.

(I Cor. 15:35-50)

10. **Will our glorified bodies be any more subject to death?**

"NEITHER CAN THEY DIE ANY MORE: for they are equal unto the angels; and are the children of God, being the children of the resurrection"—Luke 20:36.

(Rev. 20:6)

11. How should we keep our bodies from sin, since they belong to Christ?

"Now the body is not for fornication, but for the Lord; and the Lord for the body. And God hath both raised up the Lord, and will also raise up us by His own power"—I Corinthians 6:13b-14.

(Rom. 12:1; I Cor. 6:15-20; Phil. 1:20)

12. Where must all Christians appear after the resurrection at Christ's coming?

"We must all appear BEFORE THE JUDGMENT SEAT OF CHRIST; that every one may receive the things done in his body, according to that he hath done, whether it be good or bad"—II Corinthians 5:10.

(Rom. 14:10)

13. What must every Christian do before the Judgment Seat of Christ?

"So then everyone of us shall give account OF HIM-SELF to God"—Romans 14:12.

(Luke 12:1-2; I Cor. 4:5)

14. Can any true believer be condemned at the Judgment Seat of Christ?

"Verily, verily, I say unto you, He that heareth My word, and believeth on Him that sent Me, hath ever-lasting life, and SHALL NOT COME INTO CON-DEMNATION"—John 5:24.

(Rom. 8:1 ASV; I Cor. 11:32)

15. What will be the result of the judgment of the believer's works?

"If any man's work abide which he hath built there-upon, HE SHALL RECEIVE A REWARD. If any man's work shall be burned, HE SHALL SUFFER LOSS: but he himself shall be saved; yet so as by fire"—I Corinthians 3:14-15.

(I Cor. 3:8-15; Rev. 22:12)

16. What are some of the rewards which faithful Christians will receive?

"Blessed is the man that endureth temptation: for when he is tried, he shall receive THE CROWN OF LIFE, which the Lord hath promised to them that love Him"—James 1:12.

(Dan. 12:3; Matt. 10:40-42; Luke 19:12-26; II Tim. 2:12; 4:8; I Pet. 5:4)

17. How should we live and work since our works are to be judged?

"This one thing I do, forgetting those things which are behind, and reaching forth unto those things which are before, I PRESS TOWARD THE MARK FOR THE PRIZE of the high calling of God in Christ Jesus"—Philippians 3:13-14.

(I Cor. 9:22-27; Gal. 6:9; James 5:8-9; I John 2:28; Rev. 3:11)

NOTES

XXVI. THE KINGDOM

1. **What did Isaiah prophesy about the birth of Christ and His Kingdom?**

   "For unto us A CHILD is born, unto us A SON is given: and the government shall be upon His shoulder . . . Of the increase of His government and peace there shall be no end, UPON THE THRONE OF DAVID, and upon his kingdom"—Isaiah 9:6-7.
   (Mic. 5:2)

2. **Was our Lord Jesus Christ born a King?**

   "Now when Jesus was born in Bethlehem of Judea in the days of Herod the king, behold, there came wise men from the East to Jerusalem, saying, Where is He that is BORN KING OF THE JEWS?"—Matthew 2:1-2.
   (Luke 1:31-32; John 18:37)

3. **How did our Lord announce His Kingdom at His first coming?**

   "Jesus came into Galilee, preaching the Gospel of the Kingdom of God, and saying, The time is fulfilled, and the Kingdom of God is AT HAND; repent ye, and believe the gospel"—Mark 1:14-15.
   (Matt. 4:17. 23; 10:5-7; Luke 10:1, 9; 19:29-40 with Zech. 9:9)

4. **Why did not Christ set up His Kingdom over men on earth at His first coming?**

   "But they cried out, Away with Him, away with Him, crucify Him. Pilate saith unto them, Shall I crucify your King? The chief priests answered, We have no king but Caesar"—John 19:15.
   (Luke 19:14; John 1:10-11; 5:43; 10:24-25)

5. **Did God know that His Son would be rejected by men at His first coming?**

   "Him, being delivered by the determinate counsel and FOREKNOWLEDGE OF GOD, ye have taken,

and by wicked hands have crucified and slain"
—Acts 2:23.

(Matt. 16:21; Acts 3:17-21; 15:18; I Pet. 1:10-11)

6. **When will Christ take the throne of His kingdom and reign on earth?**

"When the Son of Man shall COME IN HIS GLORY, and all the holy angels with Him, THEN shall He sit upon the throne of His glory"—Matthew 25:31.

(Mark 14:60-62; Luke 19:11-15; Rev. 19:11-16)

7. **Will the coming Kingdom of our Lord extend over all nations?**

"He shall have dominion also from sea to sea, and from the River unto the ends of the earth. They that dwell in the wilderness shall bow before Him . . . Yea, all kings shall fall down before Him; ALL NATIONS shall serve Him"—Psalm 72:8-11.

(Ps. 2:6-8; Dan. 7:13-14; Zech. 14:9)

8. **What city will be the capital of Christ's coming Kingdom?**

"And many people shall go and say, Come ye, and let us go up to the Mountain of the Lord, to the House of the God of Jacob; and He will teach us of His ways, and we will walk in His paths; for out of Zion shall go forth the law, and the word of the Lord FROM JERUSALEM"—Isaiah 2:3.

(Isa. 24:23; Jer. 3:17; Zech. 8:3, 22)

9. **How will Christ rule over the nations in His Kingdom?**

"Behold, the days come, saith the Lord, that I will raise unto David a righteous Branch, and a King shall reign and prosper, and shall EXECUTE JUDG-MENT AND JUSTICE IN THE EARTH . . . And this is his name whereby He shall be called, THE LORD OUR RIGHTEOUSNESS"—Jeremiah 23:5-6.

(Isa. 11:1-5; 16:5 ASV; 32:1-2; 33:22; 40:10-11; Rev. 19:15)

10. **What did Christ promise about His people reigning with Him in the Kingdom?**

"To him that overcometh will I grant to sit with Me in My throne, even as I also overcame, and am set down with My Father in His throne"—Revelation 3:21.

(Luke 22:28-30; II Tim. 2:12; Rev. 2:26-27; 5:9-10)

11. **How long will Christ's people reign with Him on earth?**

"They shall be priests of God and of Christ, and shall reign with Him A THOUSAND YEARS" —Revelation 20:6.

(Rev. 20:4)

12. **What will be done with Satan at the beginning of Christ's Kingdom?**

"He laid hold on the dragon, that old serpent, which is the Devil, and Satan, and BOUND HIM a thousand years"—Revelation 20:2.

(Rev. 20:1-3)

13. **How will Christ judge the Living Nations at the beginning of His Kingdom?**

"And before Him shall be gathered all nations; and HE SHALL SEPARATE THEM one from another, as a shepherd divideth his sheep from the goats" —Matthew 25:32.

(Matt. 25:31-46; Joel 3:1-2)

14. **How will Christ destroy all forms of evil when He sets up the Kingdom?**

"The Son of Man shall SEND FORTH HIS ANGELS, and they shall gather out of His Kingdom all things that offend, and them which do iniquity; and shall cast them into a furnace of fire"—Matthew 13:41-42.

(Ps. 103:19-20; Isa. 37:33-36; Acts 12:23)

15. **How will Christ deal with the nation of Israel in the Kingdom?**

"For I will take you from among the heathen, and gather you out of all countries, and will bring you

into your own land . . . And ye shall dwell in the land that I gave to your fathers; and ye shall be My people, and I will be your God"—Ezekiel 36: 24, 28.
(Isa. 60:10-22; 61:4-6; Jer. 31:1-12, 35-37; Ezek. 20:33-38; 37:21-28)

16. **What will be some of the spiritual blessings in our Lord's Kingdom?**
"The earth shall be full of the knowledge of the Lord, as the waters cover the sea"—Isaiah 11:9b.
(Isa. 65:24; Jer. 31:33-34; Ezek. 36:25-27)

17. **What will be done about War when Christ sets up His Kingdom?**
"He shall judge among the nations, and shall rebuke many people: and they shall beat their swords into plowshares, and their spears into pruninghooks: nation shall not lift up sword against nation. NEITHER SHALL THEY LEARN WAR ANY MORE" —Isaiah 2:4.
(Ps. 72:6-7; Isa. 9:7a; Mic. 4:3; Zech. 9-10)

18. **Will every man receive what he produces in our Lord's Kingdom?**
"And they shall build houses, and inhabit them; and they shall plant vineyards, and eat the fruit of them. They shall not build, and another inhabit; they shall not plant, and another eat"—Isaiah 65: 21-22a.
(Amos 9:14; James 5:1-8)

19. **How will the poor be treated in the Kingdom of Christ?**
"For He shall deliver the needy when he crieth; the poor also, and him that hath no helper"—Psalm 72:12.
(Ps. 72:1-4, 13-14; Isa. 11:4; Luke 6:20)

20. **How will the sick and afflicted be treated under the reign of CHRIST?**
"Then the eyes of the BLIND shall be opened, and the ears of the DEAF shall be unstopped. Then shall

the LAME man leap as an hart, and the tongue of the
DUMB sing"—Isaiah 35:5-6a.

(Isa. 29:18; 33:24; 65:20a, 23; Matt. 11:2-5)

21. **How will even the animals be changed when Christ reigns?**

"The wolf also shall dwell with the lamb, and the
leopard shall lie down with the kid; and the calf and
the young lion and the fatling together; and a little
child shall lead them"—Isaiah 11:6.

(Isa. 11:7-9; 65:25; Ezek. 34:25, 28)

22. **How will the earth produce bountifully under Christ's rule?**

"The wilderness and the solitary place shall be glad
for them; and the desert shall rejoice, and blossom as
the rose. It shall blossom abundantly"—Isaiah
35:1-2a.

(Psa. 67:4-6; 72:16; Isa. 32:15; Amos 9:13)

23. **How will our Lord enforce His law when He reigns on earth?**

"And it shall be, that whoso will not come up of all
the families of the earth unto Jerusalem to worship
the King, the Lord of hosts, even UPON THEM
SHALL BE NO RAIN"—Zechariah 14:17.

(Zech. 14:16-19; Ps. 2:1-12; Rev. 19:15)

24. **Will our Lord's reign bring happiness to those who submit to it?**

"And the ransomed of the Lord shall return, and
come to Zion with songs and everlasting joy upon
their heads: THEY SHALL OBTAIN JOY AND
GLADNESS, and sorrow and sighing shall flee
away"—Isaiah 35:10.

(Psalms 96 and 98)

25. **What will Christ do with His Kingdom when the Thousand Years are finished?**

"Then cometh the end, when HE SHALL HAVE

DELIVERED UP THE KINGDOM TO GOD, EVEN
THE FATHER; when He shall have put down all rule
and all authority and power. For He must reign, till
He hath put all enemies under His feet"
—I Corinthians 15:24-25.
(Phil. 2:10-11)

26. How did our Lord teach His disciples to pray about the Kingdom?

"THY KINGDOM COME. Thy will be done IN
EARTH, as it is in heaven"—Matthew 6:10.

NOTES

XXVII. RESURRECTION AND JUDGMENT

(For Unbelievers)

1. **Will the dead bodies of the wicked ever be raised from the grave?**

   "ALL that are in the tombs shall hear His voice, and shall come forth . . . THEY THAT HAVE DONE EVIL, unto the resurrection of judgment"—John 5:28-29 ASV.

2. **When will the resurrection of the wicked take place?**

   "The rest of the dead lived not again until the thousand years were finished"—Revelation 20:5.

3. **How does the Bible describe the resurrection of the wicked?**

   "And the sea gave up the dead which were in it; and death and hell delivered up the dead which were in them"—Revelation 20:13a.

4. **How will the wicked be judged when they are raised from the dead?**

   "And I saw the dead, small and great, stand before God; and the books were opened: and another book was opened, which is the book of life: and the dead were judged out of those things which were written in the books, ACCORDING TO THEIR WORKS" —Revelation 20:12.

   (Acts 17:31; Rom. 2:2, 5-6 16)

5. **Can any person be saved if judged according to works?**

   "By the WORKS of the law shall no flesh be justified"—Galatians 2:16b.

   (Rom. 3:20; 4:4-7; Eph. 2:8-9)

6. **What will become of the wicked and unbelieving after they are judged according to their works?**

"But the fearful, AND UNBELIEVING, and the abominable, and murderers, and whoremongers, and sorcerers, and idolaters, and all liars, shall have their part in the lake which burneth with fire and brimstone: which is the second death"—Revelation 21:8.

(Matt. 22:13; Mark 9:43-48; Heb. 12:29; II Pet. 3:7; Rev. 20:10, 15)

7. **How long will the punishment of the unsaved continue?**

"He that believeth not the Son shall not see life; but the WRATH OF GOD ABIDETH ON HIM"—John 3:36b.

(Matt. 25:46; Mark 3:29 ASV; 9:44, 46, 48; II Thess. 1:9; Jude 13; Rev. 14:11)

8. **Will all the unsaved suffer the same degree of punishment?**

"And that servant, which knew his Lord's will, and prepared not himself, neither did according to His will, shall be beaten with MANY STRIPES. But he that knew not, and did commit things worthy of stripes, shall be beaten with FEW STRIPES. For unto whomsoever much is given, of him shall be much required"—Luke 12:47-48.

(Matt. 11:22, 24; Acts 1:25; Rom. 2:5-6)

9. **How can the saved be happy in heaven if they know that others are lost forever?**

"And God shall wipe away all tears from their eyes"—Revelation 21:4.

(Isa. 65:17 ASV)

10. **What promise do we have that God will do right?**

"The Lord is righteous in all His ways, and holy in all His works"—Psalm 145:17.

(Gen. 18:25b; II Pet. 3:9)

XXVIII. THE NEW HEAVEN AND EARTH

1. **What will come to pass after the judgment of the wicked?**

   "And I saw A NEW HEAVEN and A NEW EARTH: for the first heaven and the first earth were passed away"—Revelation 21:1.

   (II Pet. 3:10-13; Rev. 21:5)

2. **What are some of the things not found in the new earth?**

   "And there shall be no more death, neither sorrow, nor crying, neither shall there be any more pain; for the former things are passed away"—Revelation 21:4.

   (I Cor. 15:26; Rev. 22:3a)

3. **What great city will come down from God out of heaven?**

   "And I John saw THE HOLY CITY, new Jerusalem, coming down from God out of heaven, prepared as a bride adorned for her husband"—Revelation 21:2.

   (Heb. 11:16; 12:22-23; Rev. 21:3)

4. **How does the Bible describe the Holy City?**

   "And the city was PURE GOLD, like unto clear glass . . . And the twelve gates were twelve pearls; every several gate was of one pearl; and the street of the city was pure gold, as it were transparent glass"—Revelation 21:18, 21.

   (Rev. 21:10-21)

5. **Who will be the glorious light of the Holy City?**

   "And the city bath no need of the sun, neither of the moon, to shine upon it; for the glory of God did lighten it, and THE LAMP THEREOF IS THE LAMB"—Revelation 21:23 ASV.

   (Matt. 17:1-2; I John 1:5)

6. **Who will dwell in the Holy City of God?**

   "And there came unto me one of the seven angels . . . saying, Come hither, I will show thee THE BRIDE,

THE LAMB'S WIFE. And he carried me away in the spirit to a great and high mountain, and showed me that great city, the Holy Jerusalem, descending out of heaven from God"—Revelation 21:9-10.

(John 14:2-3; Eph. 5:25-27; Rev. 3:12)

7. **Will the nations on the new earth have access to the Holy City?**

"And the nations of them which are saved shall walk in the light of it: and the kings of the earth do bring their glory and honor into it. And the gates of it shall not be shut at all by day; for there shall be no night there"—Revelation 21:24-25.

(Rev. 22:14)

8. **Who will be shut out of the Holy City?**

"And there shall in no wise enter into it anything that defileth, neither whatsoever worketh abomination, or maketh a lie; but they which are written in the Lamb's book of life"—Revelation 21:27.

(Matt. 22:13; Jude 13; Rev. 22:15)

9. **Will we find joy and happiness with our Lord in the Holy City?**

"In Thy presence is FULNESS OF JOY; at Thy right hand there are PLEASURES FOR EVERMORE" —Psalm 16:11.

(John 16:22; Jude 24; Rev. 19:7; 21:4a)

10. **Will we know each other in the Holy City?**

"For now we see through a glass, darkly; but then face to face: now I know in part; but then shall I know even as also I am known"—I Corinthians 13:12.

(I John 3:2)

11. **What will we do throughout all eternity with our Lord Jesus Christ?**

"And His servants shall SERVE HIM: and they shall SEE HIS FACE; and His Name shall be in their foreheads. And there shall be no night there; and they need no candle, neither light of the sun; for the Lord God giveth them light: and they shall REIGN FOR EVER AND EVER"—Revelation 22:3-5.

(Ps. 145:1-2)

12. What is the last promise and the last prayer of the Bible?

"He which testifieth these things saith, SURELY I COME QUICKLY. Amen. EVEN SO, COME, LORD JESUS"—Revelation 22:20.

NOTES